Building Your Own PC

Buying and Assembling with Confidence

Arnie Lee

Abacus

Copyright © 1999, 2000   Arnie Lee

Copyright © 1999, 2000   **Abacus Software Inc.**
5370 52nd Street SE
Grand Rapids, MI 49512
www.abacuspub.com

Printed in the United States of America

ISBN 1-55755-355-6

10 9 8 7 6 5 4 3

Acknowledgments

Thanks to Scott, who turned plain text into a very
readable book.

Thanks to Melinda, who drew some top-notch
illustrations for this book on short notice.

Thanks to Jim, who added a lot of "usability"
suggestions to the text.

Thanks to Rachel and Michael and Jennifer and
Karla, who helped at many of the computer shows
where we "researched" this project.

And thanks to the rest of the family who made it
without us for so many weekends.

Dedication

This book is dedicated to our son, Scott.

As I see it, he probably wouldn't need this book.
Instead, he'd figure out how to build one himself.

Contents

Contents

Introduction

This book is for you if -

- ❖ You'd like to build a screaming fast Pentium-class computer.

- ❖ You'd like to have advice on selecting and buying the best components.

- ❖ You'd like to have step-by-step instuctions on assembling your new PC.

- ❖ You'd like to save money.

- ❖ You'd like to be able to later upgrace your computer to keep it current.

Since you're already reading this book, you're obviously very interested in building your own PC. This book isn't your typical computer bock. This is a "roll up your sleeves and get your hands dirty" kind of book. You'll find it to be short and to the point.

The book's step-by-step instructions make it possible for you to put together your own personal computer. And you don't have to be an electronics whiz. We'll show you how to select components, connect them and install the software that you'll need to get your PC up and running.

Figure I-1 The Pentium 166 system in this minitower case has a CD-ROM and sound card. It was assembled in about an hour and is now ready for action.

The information is based on many years of experience with PCs. We've seen several generations of personal computers and many features, peripherals and devices come and go. Therefore, we've spent a lot of time and money investing in technology that turned out to be short-lived. We want to help you avoid this mistake.

Just like Archie Bunker in the classic *All in the Family* show, this book is loaded with opinions (although educated opinions, we hope). The book will show you how to build your own PC at a rock-bottom price. You'll have the satisfaction of saving money and knowing how to repair and upgrade your computer when the time comes.

There are an infinite number of ways to combine components to make a personal computer. But this book shows you how to build a PC based on the AMD K6-2 processor. If you've been keeping up with the latest technology, you'll know that Cyrix makes a chip known as the M II. The Cyrix M II and recent Pentium variations (but not the Pentium II) are equivalent and interchangeable with the processor in this book. (The Pentium II is discussed in its own chapter because it requires a different architecture.)

Of course there are other choices. For example, you can find good buys on Intel 486 CPUs and AMD or Cyrix 586 processors. But we believe that in today's fast changing marketplace the smartest choice is with the newer, faster chips. And with all the power sitting in your new system, you'll be able to run any of today's power-hungry Windows applications with ease.

How much can you save? Unfortunately, we can't give you an exact answer. The amount of money that you save depends on many factors:

- ❖ The features you want in your custom-built computer.

- ❖ The quality of the components you select.

- ❖ The amount of time you spend shopping for these components.

- ❖ The competitiveness of the personal computer marketplace.

- ❖ How well you can bargain with salespeople.

For the computer that we're putting together in this book, we saved several hundred dollars compared to one with similar features that you can buy from a discount computer store. We bought components from several local computer stores, computer superstores and from vendors at many weekend computer shows. You can save even more if you are a better shopper than we are.

You won't find too many prices listed in this book because they've changed so quickly in recent months. Fortunately for all of us, they have always moved lower.

Because there are so many features and add-ons that you can build into a PC, it isn't possible to talk about every combination. Therefore, we have to draw some boundaries. For example, this book cannot show you how to build every kind of Pentium-class computer system. Instead, it will show you how to build a PC with these characteristics:

- ❖ AMD K6-2 CPU

- ❖ 3.5-inch floppy drive

- ❖ IDE hard drive

- ❖ Plug 'n' Play sound card

- ❖ IDE CD-ROM drive

- ❖ AGP video display card

- ❖ Monitor

- ❖ Windows 98

After putting this computer together, you'll have both the skills and the confidence to "upgrade" this new computer with virtually any other add-ons you may want. Another boundary in this book is that it cannot possibly cover all these peripherals here. So, if you're planning to add a modem or a tape backup, you'll be able to do so on your own.

How long does it take to build a PC? Not long at all. The computer pictured in Figure I-1 was assembled in about an hour. If you already have all the components, you can assemble your first computer in less than three hours and install the operating system in another hour. However, you'll spend more time evaluating, selecting and buying the components. The Shopping Check List in Chapter 7 will help you cut your nonassembly time to a minimum.

It's a good idea to read through this book entirely before you start building your computer. By doing this, you'll become very familiar with the way in which you'll be putting your computer together. If you have questions after reading a section of the book, you can ask one of the sales people or vendors to clarify the area which isn't crystal clear.

Well, enough introductions. Let's get going.

The Components Of A Computer

1.
The Components Of A Computer

The personal computer is a lot like an automobile. We all know that there are many different makes and models of automobiles. Some have small, economy engines and others have large, very powerful engines; some have AM/FM radios, others tape cassette decks and still others CD players; some have standard suspensions and others have heavy duty towing packages. But regardless of the options which you buy, automobiles are basically used for transportation.

Figure 1.1 Some autos are built for speed . . . . . And so are some computers

Similarly, there are many different makes and models of personal computers. Some have economy priced CPUs and others more expensive superfast CPUs; some have a minimal 4MB of memory and others are loaded with a hefty 32MB; some have low-cost 2x speed CD-ROM drives and others 20x; some have 8-bit sound cards and others 32-bit wave table sound cards. Regardless of the features, PCs are basically used to run applications.

The components which you choose to put into your PC are similar to the options which you choose for your automobile. Choosing from among different components determines how your PC performs similar to how choosing options determines how your automobile performs.

Selecting the right component is important for two reasons:

1. The choice of components ultimately determines how your PC performs.

2. The choice of components also determines how much your PC costs.

6

We're big advocates of helping you to save money. But don't try to save money at the expense of inferior quality. We'll show you how to build a quality system. Examine your budget, use a prepared shopping list and accept only straight answers to the questions that you ask a sales person. If you follow these guidelines, you'll save money and build the PC that meets your needs. Buy what you need, not what the store or vendor has to sell.

A Bare Bones Computer

Before we go any farther, let's look at the components in a "stripped down" computer. These are the minimal components that all personal computers are made from:

Case

The box or shell in which all of the other components are assembled. The case is typically made of metal, plastic or a combination of the two.

Power supply

Provides the electrical power for the other components. Most often, the power supply is included when you buy the case.

CPU (Central Processing Unit)

The CPU is the brain of the PC. Choosing a CPU is the single most important factor in how powerful your PC will be. As we stated in the Introduction, we'll be looking mainly at the AMD K6-2 in this book.

CPU cooling fan

A small unit with a fan located on top of the CPU. Its job is to remove heat and keep the CPU cool.

Motherboard

A large circuit board that "holds" most of the other components. The CPU, memory, video cards, hard, floppy and CD-ROM drives and other input/output cards fit into the motherboard.

Main memory

Small plug-in cards containing RAM (Random Access Memory) used by programs as working storage. Memory is often called SIMMs. This stands for <u>S</u>ingle <u>I</u>nline <u>M</u>emory <u>M</u>odule which is a fancy name for the way in which the memory is packaged on small circuit boards.

Video display card

A small plug-in card containing specialized chips that generate the signals for displaying text and graphics on the video monitor.

Monitor

The video display, resembling a television, on which the text and graphics appear.

I/O card

Another small plug-in card containing the electronics for controlling the hard drives, floppy drives, communication ports, printer port and game port. There are two major types of I/O cards: IDE and SCSI. In this book, we'll refer only to IDE controllers and not the higher performance (and more expensive) SCSI controllers.

Floppy drive

This device reads and writes from/to floppy disks.

Keyboard

This device lets you type information into the computer.

Many readers have the notion that assembling a computer is very complex. In fact, it's not at all complex. To show you that it's actually quite simple, we assembled the computer system in Figure 1.2 on the top of a table so you can see that there are very few "connections" involved. We used all of the components listed above (except for the case) to make this "bare bones" computer system.

Figure 1.2 We "built" this computer on the top of a table.
It runs as well as a computer that you'd build inside a case.

This is a real working computer system and runs just like one enclosed in a case. We don't however, recommend that you build your computer on a tabletop. One of the hazards of doing this is that it's very easy to short circuit the motherboard or one of the add-on cards when you don't have a computer case to protect the other components. Short circuiting a delicate component will probably ruin it.

Figure 1.3 (below) shows the connections between the components.

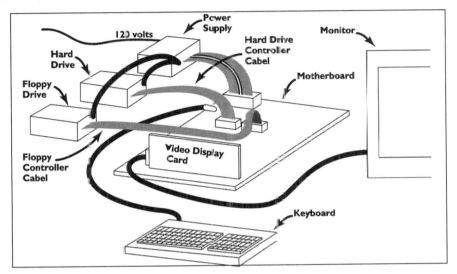

Figure 1.3 This diagram shows how the components in Figure 1.2 are connected

A State Of The Art "Screamer"

Of course none of you will be very satisfied with a bare bones PC. To turn this basic machine into a "state of the art" computer, you can add the features we've listed below (among others). These components will turn a basic PC into a real screamer:

Cache memory

This is either a small card or several small chips that act as an ultrafast path for moving data between the CPU and main memory.

Hard drive

This device holds megabytes (millions of bytes) or gigabytes (billions of bytes) of information. A hard drive not only has more capacity than a floppy drive, but reads and writes data dozens of times faster.

CD-ROM drive

This device reads CD-ROMs, circular plastic discs, that are used to hold programs and information. CD-ROMs provide an economical and convenient way to distribute large programs and huge amounts of data.

Sound card

A sound card is a plug-in card that can capture, digitize and playback sound. The sound may be music, voices or effects in either monaural or stereo.

Speakers

Similar or identical to audio stereo speakers for amplifying and/or playing the digitized sound generated by a sound card.

Modem

A modem is a plug-in card (or in the case of an external modem, a small box) that converts digital information into a form that can be sent over ordinary telephone lines. A modem is used to connect one computer to another computer in different locations.

Tape backup

This is a backup device that uses small plastic tape cartridges to store data that is originally written to the hard drive. By copying or backing up the data from the hard drive to the tape cartridge, the data is saved in case the original data on the hard drive is destroyed.

Mouse

A mouse is small hand device used to interact with the graphical user interfaces such as Windows 95 and Windows 98.

Other peripherals

There are many other peripherals or devices that you can attach to your PC. These includes printers, scanners, zip drives, bar code readers and the list goes on. Installing most of these other peripherals is straightforward and has little to do with building your PC. Therefore, we'll leave it to others to explain.

2

Selecting The Right Components

2 Selecting The Right Components

Selecting components is probably the single most confusing and time-consuming part of building your PC. There are many factors to consider when buying components. You may be bewildered by the myriad of choices in every category. Try not to feel overwhelmed. We're going to point you in the right direction.

Here are some of the factors to consider when you buy the components to build your computer:

The CPU

The single most important factor determining the performance of your PC is the CPU you choose. Basically, there are two categories of CPUs: those made by Intel and those made by other manufacturers.

A word of warning: Wherever you shop for components, you'll find bargain priced 486 CPUs. Why not buy a 486? The answer is simple. Why should you invest in yesterday's technology? Forget the 486s and go for a Pentium-class CPU.

You can choose a CPU from the following list today:

- ❖ Intel Pentium
- ❖ Intel Pentium Pro
- ❖ Intel Pentium II
- ❖ Intel Pentium MMX
- ❖ AMD K5
- ❖ AMD K6
- ❖ Cyrix 6x86
- ❖ Cyrix 6x86MX
- ❖ AMD K6-2
- ❖ Cyrix M II
- ❖ Pentuim III
- ❖ AMD K7

Since these processors all have varying features, capabilities and operating speeds, you can easily be confused when choosing one for your own PC. We'll try to make selecting a processor easier for you. Selecting a CPU is merely a trade-off between price and performance.

The power rating of a CPU is based on its "clock speed." The clock speed of a CPU is measured in "megahertz" (or MHz), which stands for millions of cycles per second—pretty darn fast. The work a CPU performs is paced by the speed of its internal clock. In other words, the faster the clock runs, the more work the CPU can do. This in turn creates a more powerful computer. As you would expect, the more powerful CPUs cost more.

Figure 2.1 The bottom and top sides of a new Pentium MMX chip, the "engine" of your computer. The CPU on the right is a Pentium 'clone' made by Cyrix. For all intents and purposes, it runs just like a Pentium.

As we go to press again (September 1999), the typical "starter system" is powered by at least a 350MHz CPU. You can of course find systems that use less than a 350MHz chip, but the 350MHz is typical in starter systems. Table 2.2 lists the street prices of Pentium CPUs through the fourth quarter 1999. These prices will most certainly change downward eventually, but the table shows that for a few additional dollars, you get an incremental increase in performance.

Table 2.2	
Street prices of Pentium CPUs (4th quarter, 1999)	
Intel CPU	Street Price
Pentium MMX 233MHz	$45
Pentium II 350	$170
Pentium II 500	$275

Intel introduced the Intel MMX CPUs in early 1997. MMX is a new technology developed by Intel to increase the speed performance of certain types of popular applications, especially multimedia and graphics applications. Most applications don't take advantage of the speed enhancements, but games, drawing, video and similar applications will get a boost. (See the information specific to the MMX on the following pages.)

Discovering the difference in CPUs

Basically, we can divide the CPUs into four groups:

1. Pentium-compatible CPUs
   Include the Intel Pentium, AMD K5 and Cyrix 6x86

2. MMX-compatible CPUs
Include the Intel Pentium MMX, AMD's K6 and K6-2 and Cyrix's 6x86MX and M II

3. Pentium Pro CPUs
Optimized for full 32-bit applications such as Windows NT (require a special motherboard).

4. Pentium II CPUs
Combines the 32-bit performance of Pentium Pro, improved performance with 16-bit applications and MMX compatibility. These also require a special motherboard. Performance of the K6-2 and M II compares well against the P II, without requiring a special motherboard.

Since the Pentium Pro and Pentium II CPUs both require special motherboards, we're not considering either for *Building Your Own PC*.

Instead, we've confined our discussion to CPUs that are "Socket 7-compatible"—meaning that all these CPUs will fit on a motherboard which has a Socket 7. When you buy a motherboard, make certain to ask the dealer if it's compatible with the CPU that you want to buy. If you purchase a late-manufactured motherboard, it will be compatible with the Intel Pentium and Pentium MMX, AMD K5 and K6 and Cyrix 6x86 and Cyrix 6x86MX CPUs. The latest CPUs, the K7 and Pentium III, may have needs not met by earlier boards.

You can ask the following questions:

Does the Socket 7 have pinouts for P55C?
The Intel Pentium MMX, AMD K6 and K6-2, and Cyrix 6x86MX and M II CPUs are P55C processors. The pinouts are different from the older P54C pinouts used by the Intel Pentium, AMD K5 and Cyrix 6x86 CPUs.

Does the motherboard support dual voltage?
For example, some processors use 2.8 volts for the processor core and 3.1 volts for the input/output. The motherboard has jumpers to independently set these specifications.

Does the motherboard have a BIOS to support the new CPUs?
You'll want to make sure that the new processors are recognized by the BIOS.

Intel Pentium MMX CPUs

The Intel Pentium MMX CPUs are 10%-15% faster than their Pentium counterparts. Since MMX CPUs are usually interchangeable with non-MMX CPUs on the motherboard, the cost for the gain in performance is a factor of the CPU price alone. MMX CPUs are up to 50% faster if the applications have been optimized to used the new MMX instructions. But to take advantage of the speed, you must upgrade your software to MMX versions when they're available.

A CPU with MMX has 57 additional instructions not found in a standard Pentium CPU. These MMX instructions process multiple data simultaneously (in parallel) making some applications run faster. Intel refers to this as Single Instruction Multiple Data. In particular, multimedia applications that perform repetitive operations on small chucks of data are best able to take advantage of these new instructions. In fact, many suggest that the term "MMX" is shorthand for "multimedia."

When optimized for these MMX instructions, the application can run up to 50% faster. Software companies have been moving very quickly to update their programs to use MMX technology, and this transition will continue since all of the new CPUs are MMX compatible.

The Intel MMX CPUs have several improvements compared to the standard Pentiums:

* 57 MMX instructions
* 16K code cache
* 16K data cache
* Improved branch prediction
* Improved pipeline
* Large write buffers
* Socket 7 compatible

AMD's Athlon

Formerly known as the K-7 processor, Athlon is a major threat to Intel's position as the CPU market leader. The Athlon surpasses the Pentium III in nearly every benchmark test. The Athlon's top production speed at press time is 650MHz, though non-production models have already reached 1GHz (one gigaherz). The 512K L2 cache running at half of the Athlon's core clock speed is the same as the PIII's, though it has the capacity for up to an 8MB L2 cache that runs at full core clock speed. The 64KB L1 cache is four times the size of the PIII's. The Athlon uses a Slot A connection to the motherboard, which is cosmetically similar to (but technically different than) Intel's Slot 1 architecture. Featuring MMX and 3Dnow! technology and performing in a very stable manner, the Athlon is the choice for power-hungry builders.

AMD K6 CPUs

The K6 is made by AMD. Like the Cyrix 6x86MX, the K6 is also MMX compatible.

Although it is pin-compatible with the Intel Pentium MMX CPUs, AMD has claimed that the K6 CPU performs better than the Intel Pentium Pro CPUs. Independent tests have suggested that the AMD-K6 does deliver better performance than the Pentium Pro for some types of processing. And since the K6 is compatible with standard Pentium motherboards (Socket 7 compatible), the overall cost of a K6 computer system is less than a Pentium Pro system.

The K6s are a very attractive alternative to the Intel and Cyrix processors. Some of the features which account for the K6's performance are:

- Integrated 64K Cache Unit

- Large TLB enhances cache performance

- Large branch prediction buffer

- MMX compatible with Intel MMX processors

- Socket 7 compatible

AMD K6-2

An even better choice is the K6-2. It works with a 100MHz system bus and will run up to 475MHz. It features an internal L2 cache operating at the same frequency as the processor. It uses the standard socket 7 motherboard (and the soon-to-be-standard Super 7). It also incorporates 3-D and MMX technology and support for AGP. The K6-2 offers the biggest bang for your bucks, which is why we choose the K6-2 for the computers we built to illustrate *Building your Own PC*.

Table 2.3	
Street prices of AMD-K6 and AMD-K7 CPUs	
Intel MMX	Projected Street Price
AMD K6-2 350	$47
AMD K6-2 450	$92
AMD K6-3 450	$200
AMD K-7 350	$515

Table 2.3 on the right lists the popular K6 CPUs.

Celeron

Intel intended its Celeron line of processors to be a low-end alternative to the Pentium II. In practice, the Celeron performs nearly as well as the PII, thanks to its level-two cache memory built into the chip. It also offers MMX media enhancement technology. The main differences between the two CPUs are the size of the L2 cache and the speed of the bus clock. The PII's L2 cache is twice the size of the Celeron's. The Celeron has been limited to 66MHz bus speed, while the PII uses the newer 100MHz bus. Unless you're using resource intensive applications, you can have the same performance for a lot less money by selecting a Celeron. Celerons are currently available at speeds up to 500MHz in two configurations, Intel's Slot One and the new Socket 370 architecture, which is cosmetically similar to the Socket 7 design.

Cyrix 6x86MX CPUs

The 6x86MX is Cyrix's version of MMX. It is essentially a 6x86 processor with Intel MMX-compatible instructions. Cyrix has added several enhancements which boost the performance of the 6x86MX. These include:

- 64K Cache Unit - four times larger than 6x86 CPU

- TLB Size—three times larger than 6x86 CPU—enhances cache performance

- Voltage: 2.8V uses less power

❖ MMX: compatible with Intel MMX processors

❖ Socket 7 compatible

The prices are based on published material Cyrix has released as of the fourth quarter 1999.

Table 2.4	
Street prices of Cyrix 6x86MX CPUs	
Cyrix processor	Projected Street Price
MX-266	$26
MX-300	$30
MII-400	$60

As with the 6x86 CPUs, these are cleverly named to indicate their relative performance compared to the Intel Pentium MMX CPUs.

Cyrix M II

The M II is Cyrix's latest chip. It features MMX instructions, enhanced memory management and a 64KB internal cache. Performance of the M II ranks with Intel's much-hyped Pentium II ("M II," "P II," get it?), but the price is much friendlier and it uses a standard Socket 7 CPU socket. This is a good choice for those trying to cut budget corners.

Pentium II

Intel's response to AMD's and Cyrix's pressure is the Pentium II. The P II's innovations are more cosmetic than practical (the older Pentium Pro has better performance in most tests). Trying to distance itself from its competitors, Intel departed from the standard socket 7 motherboard design, creating the Slot One design. This means that the P II can not be used on the same type of motherboard as previous Pentium, AMD or Cyrix chips. If you decide that a P II is best for you, Chapter 4 explains the special hardware you'll need.

Pentium III

According to Intel, the Pentium III is "Intel's most advanced and powerful processor for the desktop PC." Featuring 70 new instructions, MMX and speeds up to 600 MHz, the PIII will easily handle office applications and will represent itself well when running multimedia and 3-D applications. The PIII also utilizes the Slot 1 motherboard connections.

The bottom line

The prices of CPUs have been falling quite rapidly and most industry watchers predict they'll continue to drop. But waiting for prices to fall means you won't be able to use the computer today. Our advice: don't put off that purchase. Sure, it may be cheaper tomorrow, but you'll also delay the fun, pleasure and utility of using that new computer today. So don't wait too long.

Does it matter whether you choose an Intel, AMD or Cyrix? Probably not.

Although the AMD K6 and Cyrix 6x86MX processors are relatively new, they have proven reliable and readily available. Their appearance has also coincided with steep price drops for the Intel Pentium MMX CPUs. The K6-2, M II and P II offer even more performance for a broader range of applications. The current price wars are keeping even these newest chips affordable. For the consumer, that's a great benefit. Now you have a choice at a variety of prices.

Motherboard

The motherboard is a large circuit board that accepts the CPU, memory, plug-in peripheral cards, various connectors and the supporting circuitry for the system.

The motherboard is the most crucial component you'll buy. You'll also have more questions about selecting a motherboard than any other component. There are many different makes and models of motherboards. Most are made in Taiwan, Korea or China, where the manufacturing costs are among the lowest in the world. And since so many companies make motherboards, there's a lot of competition. This means high quality and low prices, which is good for us as consumers.

*Figure 2.5 A typical Pentium motherboard like this one has
four ISA slots, four PCI slots, four 72-pin SIMM sockets and a cache socket. The large circle shows the
location of the Socket 7 CPU socket.*

How do you decide which motherboard to buy?

Note On Motherboards

The specific features provided by any motherboard are usually determined by which *chipset* is used on that motherboard. A *chipset* provides the supporting circuitry to control most of the other components on the motherboard. In earlier computers, such as the "ancient" 386, the functions of the chipset were performed by many separate integrated circuits. or chips. Each chip controlled a very specific function, such as refreshing the dynamic RAM memory or regulating the high-speed DMA transfer to and from a hard drive. In today's computers, a chipset (usually a set of two to four highly integrated chips) replaces the numerous separate chips.

The two main benefits of chipsets are:

1. The motherboards are less prone to problems
2. The motherboards are less expensive

We've listed criteria on the following pages to consider in selecting a motherboard. But as you'll see, your selection is in part predetermined by which chipset is used on any particular motherboard.

Select a motherboard that will accommodate the type and speed of your CPU

Since we've decided to use AMD's K6-2, we'll choose a motherboard that supports this CPU. Some motherboards are built to handle CPU speeds up to 133MHz. The latest motherboards can handle clock speeds of up to 200MHz. If you're looking to use an Intel MMX CPU, make sure that the motherboard can handle its 2.8 voltage requirement. The K6-2 requires 3.3 volts.

Since you're a wise shopper, buy a motherboard that will be able to work with these faster CPUs.

If you've opted for a CPU that requires a specialized connector (Slot 1, Slot A or Socket 370), be sure to choose a motherboard with that feature. Your vendor will be able to recommend the motherboards that are compatible with your CPU. If you're looking to install a Cyrix CPU, make sure that it's capable of operating at a bus speed of 75MHz.

Select a motherboard that has the type of system bus that you prefer

Almost all new motherboards use the PCI bus It is the most popular bus today because Intel has put a lot of effort into making it standard. The PCI bus is capable of transferring data 64-bit at a time at rates up to 100MHz. Besides PCI bus slots and VL-Bus slots, all motherboards also have slots for older ISA or EISA plug-in cards as well. This lets you use the "legacy" 8-bit and 16-bit ISA cards and 32-bit EISA cards in your new PC.

A typical Pentium motherboard has three or four slots for PCI or VL-Bus cards and three or four slots for ISA/EISA cards. The PCI bus is the standard for Pentium systems because it offers simplicity, wide availability of other peripheral cards and future expansion capabilities.

ATX offers power-saving enhancements

You may also want to consider an ATX motherboard. ATX, the latest motherboard specification from Intel, offers several advantages. The most obvious feature it offers to users is the ability to put a computer into "sleep" or "suspend" mode, or to completely power down via a software command. In other words, instead of turning the computer off with a power switch, a user just shuts down Windows normally, and Windows turns the computer off. ATX offers more features inside the case, such as easier access to components, lower power consumption, better cooling and the ability to use full-length add-on cards without conflicting with other components. If you opt for an ATX motherboard, be sure you also have an ATX case and power supply.

Select a motherboard based on whether you want onboard I/O

A motherboard with onboard I/O has the built-in electronics for controlling fixed drives, floppy drives, communication ports, a parallel port and usually a game port. Buying a motherboard with onboard I/O means that you won't have to buy a separate add-on board for handling the I/O. Onboard I/O also frees up one of the slots on the motherboard, a factor worth considering if your case is small or you are planning to add a lot of peripheral cards. Make sure the onboard I/O has these characteristics: EIDE (Enhanced IDE) interface capable of handling four fixed drives, two floppy drives, one parallel port and two high-speed serial communications ports using 16550 UARTs for faster, more reliable data transfer.

Select a motherboard which supports *pipeline burst cache*

Caching is a way to speed up access to main memory. Using standard cache, four bytes of data can be transferred from cache to the CPU in eight clock cycles. A special feature of the Pentiums is their ability to access memory in *burst* mode, where the same four bytes of data can be transferred in only five clock cycles. On most motherboards, the cache is already built-in. On other motherboards, the cache is added separately. The more recent separate cache is called "COAST" memory. COAST is an acronym for Cache On A Stick—a clever name for the small circuit boards which accommodate the pipeline burst cache memory. (Pentium IIs have cache built into the chip, so you don't need to worry about type or amount.)

Select a motherboard which supports the type and amount of memory that you're likely to use

Most Pentium motherboards have four sockets that accept 72-pin SIMMs. Since a single 72-pin SIMM varies in capacity from 4MB to 32MB, a motherboard with four sockets can have anywhere from 8MB (using two 4MB SIMMs) to 128MB (using four 32MB SIMMs). If you need more memory, look for a motherboard that has six or more 72-pin SIMM sockets.

Some motherboards also have sockets to accept the older 30-pin SIMMs. If you're on a tight budget and have a considerable amount of money invested in 30-pin SIMMS, then you can extend your investment in this older memory by selecting a motherboard that has sockets for both 30-pin memory *and* 72-pin memory. Otherwise, we recommend buying a motherboard that accommodates only 72-pin SIMMs.

Most Pentium motherboards can take advantage of the faster EDO memory. You should select one of these motherboards even if you aren't initially planning to use EDO memory. Many users prefer to buy non-parity memory. If you are one of those who likes the security which parity memory offers, make sure that the motherboard supports parity checking.

DIMM memory, explained more fully later uses a 168-pin connection. This is fast becoming the more popular format for RAM. Because DIMMs don't need to be installed in pairs (as SIMMs do), you don't need as many slots on the motherboard. If you decide to use DIMMs, be sure the motherboard has 168-pin connectors.

Examples of major chipsets

Following are the major chipsets used on Pentium-class motherboards. When you're selecting a motherboard, you can easily know which features the motherboard supports based on which chipset is used on that motherboard.

Acer Labs Aladdin chipset (www.ali.com.tw)

❖ PCI bus only with ISA support

❖ I/O onboard

❖ Keyboard controller

❖ Up to 1MB of write-back pipeline burst cache

❖ Parity and non-parity memory up to 768MB; supports EDO memory

Intel 430 FX chipset (http://www.intel.com/design/chipsets/index.htm)

❖ PCI bus with ISA support

❖ I/O onboard for up to four IDE devices

❖ Pipeline burst cache

❖ Non-parity only memory up to 128MB; supports EDO memory

❖ Power management

Intel 430 HX chipset http://www.intel.com/design/chipsets/index.htm)

❖ PCI bus with ISA support

❖ I/O onboard for up to four IDE drives

❖ Pipeline burst cache

❖ Parity and non-parity memory up to 512MB; supports EDO memory

❖ Power management

❖ Universal Serial Bus support

Intel 430 VX chipset (http://www.intel.com/design/chipsets/index.htm)

❖ PCI bus with ISA support

❖ I/O onboard for up to four IDE drives

❖ Pipeline burst cache

❖ Memory access about 10%-15% faster than Triton FX chipset

❖ Parity and non-parity memory up to 128MB; supports EDO memory; supports synchronous DRAM

❖ Power management

❖ Universal Serial Bus support

Intel 430 TX chipset (http://www.intel.com/design/chipsets/index.htm)

❖ PCI bus with ISA support

❖ I/O onboard for up to four IDE drives

❖ Pipeline burst cache

❖ Supports up to 256 MB of parity/non-parity, EDO and SDRAM

Intel 440 FX (http://www.intel.com/design/chipsets/index.htm)

❖ PCI bus with ISA support

❖ I/O onboard for up to four IDE drives

❖ Supports up to one gigabyte of RAM, EDO and SDRAM

Intel 440 LX (http://www.intel.com/design/chipsets/index.htm)

❖ PCI bus with ISA support

❖ I/O onboard for up to four IDE drives

❖ Supports up to one gigabyte of EDO RAM or 512MB of SDRAM

❖ Support for AGP

Opti Viper chipset (http://www.opti.com/html/products.html)

❖ PCI bus and VL bus with ISA support

❖ I/O onboard

❖ Up to 2MB of write-back pipeline burst cache

❖ Parity and non-parity memory up to 512MB; supports EDO memory

SIS chipset (http://www.sis.com.tw)

❖ PCI bus and VL bus

❖ I/O onboard for up to four IDE devices

❖ Pipeline burst cache

❖ 2MB of write-back cache

❖ Parity and non-parity memory up to 512MB; supports EDO memory

❖ Power management

We have just seen how selecting a chipset eliminates many of the decisions that we have to make in selecting a motherboard. However, there are a few other things to consider. You should select a motherboard that has a BIOS from one of the major manufacturers. The BIOS is a small chip which contains the most important program instructions for initializing and testing the computer at startup, setting the Plug 'n' Play devices and handling the computer's basic functions for inputting and outputting data, for example. We recommend a motherboard that has a Plug 'n' Play *Flash BIOS*. A flash BIOS includes a chip that is reprogrammable, meaning the functions can be easily updated at a later time using a program supplied by the manufacturer. The program is usually supplied on a diskette when you buy the motherboard. The major BIOS manufacturers are AMI (American Megatrends International), Award, DTK, Microid Research and Phoenix.

Plug 'n' Play

Plug 'n' Play's goal is to automatically detect and configure new peripherals in a computer system. When the BIOS and operating system recognize a new Plug 'n' Play peripheral, they can automatically decide how to configure the IRQs, DMAs and other technical specifications. Plug 'n' Play requires that the BIOS, operating system and peripheral device all meet the Plug 'n' Play standard.

Select a motherboard that has a built-in mouse port. If your motherboard doesn't have a mouse port, then you'll either have to use one of the computer's two serial ports or buy a separate add-on card to add a mouse to your computer system.

Another convenient feature to look for is a built-in game port. But don't be too critical if the motherboard doesn't have a built-in game port. Most sound cards include a game port, and since you'll probably want a sound card in your PC, you'll also get a game port at the same time.

Some motherboards are better laid out than others. For example, we've found motherboards that cannot use a full-length add-on card because it won't fit into the slot without interfering with one or more of the other components on the motherboard. Check the layout to assure yourself that this won't be a problem.

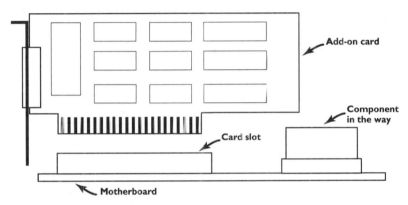

Figure 2.11 This add-in card cannot be fully inserted into the slot because the component already on the motherboard is in the way.

To make their products more attractive, some manufacturers have added other features to their motherboards:

❖ Built-in video display card

❖ Built-in sound card

❖ Built-in SCSI I/O adapter

We recommend when you're building a flexible system to select a motherboard that does not have any of these additional features. While the price of a motherboard with a built-in video display card or sound card may be attractive, you lose some of the flexibility in future upgrades. Instead, we recommend separate plug-in cards that perform these particular functions. By taking this approach, you'll build a system that can be easily upgraded at a later time.

Special Tip

Don't buy a motherboard without the user's manual. The user's manual has very specific and necessary instructions for setting the various jumpers and switches. Configuring your motherboard is one of the most critical steps in building a trouble-free PC, and the user's manual is a required part.

Cases And Power Supplies

Selecting a case and power supply is mostly a choice of deciding which of the two major styles of case you prefer. These two styles are *desktop* and *tower*. In simplest terms, cases vary by their size, profile, and color.

As its name suggests, a desktop computer case is meant to sit on top of a desk—horizontally. A desktop case is designed so that it doesn't take up a lot of space on the desk. The downside of using this more compact desktop case is that there usually isn't a lot of room inside the case for peripherals.

Figure 2.12 An example of a desktop case.

Tower cases are meant to stand upright, either on the floor or on a shelf. There are variations to the tower cases: A full tower, a midi-tower and a mini-tower case, depending on the height of the unit. As you'd expect, the larger the case, the more space there is inside for adding components. If you're planning to build a PC with four hard drives, two floppies and lots of add-ons, you should buy a full tower case.

Whether you buy a desktop or a tower, the case most likely includes the power supply. The power supply produces a regulated source of electricity—meaning that the voltage doesn't vary. Power supplies have electrical connectors that supply the motherboard and other devices with +5V, -5V and +12V. A power supply is rated by the number of watts of power it can deliver to all connected devices. Earlier computers could easily use up to 200 watts of power. But the components used by today's computers are much more energy efficient, and we haven't seen a computer in a long time requiring that much power. Most power supplies are rated for 230 watts or more so there's a safety margin in the event you need a little extra power.

If you choose an ATX motherboard, be sure to choose an ATX case (and matching power supply).

Most tower cases and some desktop cases also include a cooling fan. This fan removes the heat inside the enclosed case. Excessive heat can cause premature failure of the components. New CPUs generate considerably more heat than their 486 predecessors. While you may not like its continuous hum, it's a good idea to choose a case—desktop or tower—with a cooling fan.

Besides the power connectors, several other connectors will be attached to various components in the computer. These may include connectors for the power indicator, turbo switch, hard drive LED and built-in speaker.

Make sure that the case you select includes a small box or plastic bag containing the mounting and accessory hardware. These include various-size screws, washers, brackets and standoffs that are essential in assembling your computer.

Figure 2.13 This is an example of a tower case.

Memory

A computer's main memory, or RAM, is built from small circuit boards called SIMMs. Pentium motherboards are designed to use standard 72-pin SIMMs. If you count the "fingers" on the bottom edge of a SIMM, you'll see why it is called a 72-pin module.

Figure 2.14 Example of a 72-pin SIMM.

Most Pentium motherboards have four 72-pin sockets. The four sockets are organized as two banks of two sockets each. These are identified as Bank 0 and Bank 1. By design, both sockets in a bank must contain SIMMs; therefore you must add SIMMs to the motherboard in pairs; you cannot add a single SIMM at a time. Bank 0 must be filled before Bank 1. For a 32MB system, you can use two 16MB SIMMs in Bank 0 or four 8MB SIMMs in both Bank 0 and Bank 1.

Figure 2.15 This motherboard has four 72-pin SIMM sockets.

When you're buying memory, you may see it advertised with a lot of technical numbers. Here's an example of an advertisement for memory:

4MB 1x32 60ns 72-pin SIMMs w/EDO	$10
8MB 2x32 60ns 72-pin SIMMs w/EDO	$20
16MB 4x36 60ns 72-pin SIMMs w/parity	$36
32MB 8x32 60ns 72-pin SIMMs	$50

Figure 2.16 Here's a sample of how you might see memory advertised.

To help you understand what this all means, let's decode some of this jargon. When you select RAM, you have to specify several characteristics:

❖ **Amount of memory on the SIMM**
Represents the amount of RAM that the module adds to your computer. The amount is stated in MB (for millions of bytes).

❖ **Arrangement of chips on the SIMM**
Describes the way in which the individual chips are accessed on the SIMM. For our purposes, you can consider this value to be another way of describing the amount of memory on the SIMM listed in Table 2.17 on the right.

Table 2.17	
Arrangement	Capacity
1X32 or 1X36	4MB
2X32 or 2X36	8MB
4X32 or 4X36	16MB
8X32 or 8X36	32MB

❖ **Time to access data**
Represents the amount of time required to access any piece of data within the SIMM. The time is represented in *ns* (for *nanoseconds,* which is one-billionth of a second!). In the above examples, the 4MB SIMM has a speed of 70 nanoseconds while the 8MB SIMM has a 60 nanosecond speed. For CPUs 120MHz and above, use 60ns SIMMs or faster. You can "mix" two SIMMs of different speed, for example 70ns and 60ns SIMMs. However, the access speed will be the slower of the pair, 70ns in this case.

❖ **Parity or non-parity**

Determines whether a SIMM has parity checking. Parity checking is a way to make a computer's memory more reliable. Without parity checking a byte of RAM is composed of 8 bits of memory; with parity checking a byte of RAM is made up of 9 bits of memory. The extra bit is a "check" bit which is used to make sure that the data in the remaining 8 bits is valid. If you see the designation 1x36 or 2x36 or 4x36 or 8x36, then you'll know that this is a SIMM with parity bits.

❖ **EDO or non-EDO**

EDO stands for <u>Ex</u>tended <u>Data</u> <u>O</u>ut and is a newer type of SIMM that is 10 to 15 percent faster than conventional SIMMs. An EDO SIMM fits in all motherboards that accept 72-pin SIMMs. However, the faster access time is available only if the motherboard is designed specifically to use EDO SIMMs. Most that you'll find today are EDO ready.

❖ **SDRAM**

SDRAM is a new type of high-speed RAM, faster than EDO. If you opt for SDRAM, be sure it is supported by your motherboard.

Always buy SIMMs in pairs. Most memory specialists recommend that both SIMMs in a pair be made by the same manufacturer. For the small difference in price between EDO and non-EDO SIMMs, we recommend that you go with the EDO type or SDRAM and enjoy the performance gain. A 32MB system is the minimum that we recommend to take advantage of the K6-2's power, especially if you're planning to run Windows 95. You can try to get away with less, but we don't think you'll be happy with an under-performing PC. Regardless of what Microsoft says, Win 95 users should have at least 32 MB of RAM, and if you can afford it, go for 64 MB. You'll notice the difference.

Special Note
Many Pentium motherboards sold today use non-parity SIMMs. Make sure that the memory you buy matches the type of memory supported by the motherboard. If you're building a PC that absolutely requires the utmost in uptime and data security, choose a motherboard that uses parity memory.

Modern motherboards are slowly replacing SIMMs with DIMMs (Dual Inline Memory Modules). These DIMM chips have 168 pins along the connector and don't have to be installed in pairs. Most Pentium II boards only accept DIMMs.

Table 2.18	
Street prices of DIMMs	
32MB 8ns SDRAM DIMM PC-100	$38
64MB 8ns SDRAM DIMM PC-100	$80
128MB 8ns SDRAM DIMM PC-100	$150
256MB 8ns SDRAM DIMM PC-100	$325

Video Display Cards

Selecting a good video display card is critical to making your PC perform well. K6-2s are very powerful and the amount of data that these CPUs can process is considerable. Most of you will use either Windows 95 or Windows 98. This graphical interface "draws" tremendous amounts of text to the screen by way of the video display card. A slow video display card can *waste* the speed of a fast Pentium CPU.

Earlier PCs were designed around the classic 16-bit ISA (Industry Standard Association) bus or the later 32-bit EISA (Extended ISA) bus. This limited pathway to the video card was therefore a bottleneck to fast video performance. If you're thinking about using an older ISA-bus video display card, DON'T. Today's newer VL-bus or PCI video display cards offer a tremendous performance gain over the ISA video display cards.

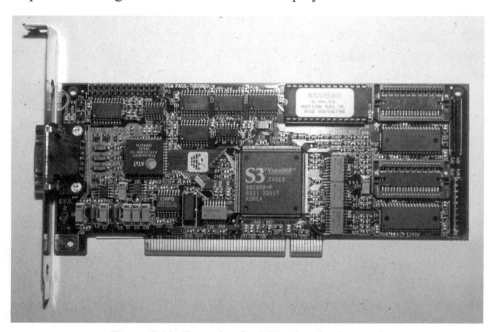

Figure 2.19 Example of a PCI video display card.

The VL-Bus (VESA Local bus) was designed to improve the video performance of ISA systems by moving data between the CPU and the video display card at a much faster speed. Today, both the PCI and VLB system bus on motherboards provides a wider, streamlined pathway for the video data, which greatly improves the overall PC performance. Don't try to save money by buying an older generation video display card. Instead, buy a PCI or VLB video display card (matching the system bus of your motherboard).

We'll repeat some earlier advice again. The PCI bus is now the standard for Pentiums. We recommend a PCI motherboard and video display card.

However, if you're hungry for the latest and greatest system with the best performance, you should look into an AGP video board. AGP (Accelerated Graphics Port) is the newest high-speed data bus for graphics cards. AGP moves more data at a faster speed. It accomplishes this through several means. First, it offers more bandwidth than PCI, up to four times more. In laymen's terms, it has a fatter data pipe, allowing more data to move faster. Second, AGP devices don't need to share this bandwidth; every PCI device in your computer shares the same limited amount of PCI bandwidth. Lastly, AGP video cards are able to store 3-D textures in the computer's main memory, allowing larger textures. Although AGP won't truly shine without 100MHz motherboards and new OSes, both of these are already shipping. If you decide to get an AGP video card, be sure you also have an AGP motherboard.

When selecting a video display card, you should pay attention to the type and amount of memory for the card. These two factors determine the display speed and maximum display resolution of the card. There are three types of memory: DRAM, VRAM and WRAM. DRAM is the same type of memory as the computer system's main memory. A card with DRAM is less expensive to buy than the same card with VRAM. A video display card with VRAM can generate the display faster. VRAM is "dual-ported"—there are two paths to the same memory location. This second path lets the video circuitry access the VRAM at the same time as the CPU so that neither one has to wait for the other. WRAM is also dual-ported, but it is better organized so that it's faster and cheaper to produce than VRAM.

A video display card with more memory can operate at a higher resolution. If you're planning to run only word processing or accounting applications on your PC, then 2MB of video memory may be sufficient. But more highly graphical applications, such as CAD, games or desktop publishing, need a card with at least 4MB of video memory. Keep in mind that the maximum resolution of the card can be achieved only if your monitor is capable of displaying that resolution.

Well-known manufacturers of video display cards include:

❖ ATI	❖ Cirrus Logic	❖ Diamond
❖ Genoa	❖ Hercules	❖ Matrox
❖ Number Nine	❖ Orchid	❖ Trident

Monitors

In selecting a monitor, remember that not all monitors are created equal. The major factors to consider are the screen size, dot pitch, refresh rate, interlace, maximum resolution and energy saving features.

The most economical monitors are 14" in size. If you spend a lot of time (two or more hours a day) using the computer, you'll appreciate a 15" or 17" monitor. Some users such as graphic artists and CAD users may even want to consider a 21" monitor. A larger screen is certainly easier on the eyes.

The characters and graphics on a color monitor are formed by a set of three-color *triads*. The dot pitch is a measure of the spacing between adjacent triads. When this measure is smaller, the characters and graphics appear "tighter" or sharper to the eye. Less expensive monitors have a dot pitch of .35 or .38 mm. We recommend a monitor with a dot pitch of .28 mm or smaller. Some of the more expensive monitors have a dot pitch of .25 mm.

The refresh rate is the frequency at which the characters and graphics are redrawn on the screen. The higher the frequency, the less the image appears to flicker. For flicker-free viewing, the refresh rate should be about 80-85 Hz, or 80-85 times a second. Almost all monitors today have a multisync feature. This means that they are able to adjust their refresh rate within a range of values to match the signals that the video display card outputs to the monitor.

A monitor redraws the screen using an electron gun. This gun shoots a beam at the inside of the screen from the left side to the right in lines starting at the top to the bottom. A monitor is designed to operate in one of two ways: interlace or non-interlace mode. In non-interlace mode, the screen is painted from top to bottom by an electron beam in a single pass. Monitors that operate in interlace mode paint the screen in two passes. The odd number lines are redrawn during the first pass and the even numbers are redrawn during the second pass. The time to redraw the entire screen is identical in either mode. However, less expensive monitors use interlace mode since they can be designed to operate at lower refresh rates. Non-interlace monitors appear to have a more stable image, but may cost a bit more. For highest quality, choose a non-interlace monitor.

The maximum resolution is the number of individually addressable pixels that the monitor is capable of displaying. We recommend that you select a monitor that has a resolution of at least 1024 x 768 pixels. Many monitors can display up to 1280 x 1024 pixels, but they may cost more. Keep in mind that a monitor's maximum resolution cannot be achieved unless the video display card is capable of operating at that resolution as well.

A monitor is one of the heaviest consumers of electrical power. Newer energy saving monitors are capable of going to "sleep" when the computer is sitting idle for a length of time. A computer's video display card must send and the monitor must be capable of responding to a DPMS (Display Power Management Signal). Selecting an energy saving monitor can save from $25 to $75 a year in electrical costs.

Some of the brand names in monitors include:

- ❖ Acer
- ❖ Hitachi
- ❖ NEC
- ❖ Princeton
- ❖ Samtron
- ❖ Sony
- ❖ Viewsonic
- ❖ Zenith
- ❖ Samsung

CPU Cooling Fan

A K6-2 CPU has in the neighborhood of 3 million transistors jam packed into a package about 2" x 2" in size. Talk about crowded! All those busy electrons racing around inside a small ceramic square create a lot of heat. A K6-2 uses almost 20 watts of energy, so we strongly recommend that you use a cooling fan to remove the heat from the CPU.

A cooling fan is actually made of two parts: the heat sink and the fan. The heat sink is a square metal plate that sits on top of the CPU. The fan housing clips over the top of the metal plate and locks the assembly in place. The connectors on the fan are then connected to either a motherboard connector or a power supply connector.

Figure 2.20 This CPU cooling fan will keep the Pentium running cool.

Although this book is about building a K6-2 computer, the Cyrix and most Pentium CPUs are plug compatible with the K6-2. We expect that some computer builders may choose to use these very capable (and the Cyrixes are competitively priced) CPUs on their motherboards.

Another word of caution: the Cyrix CPUs require about 22 watts of power, and therefore generate significantly more heat than a Pentium. If you install a Cyrix CPU, make sure that you install a quality CPU cooling fan.

> **Special Tip**
>
> Do yourself a favor...don't run a Pentium CPU without a cooling fan.

I/O Card

I/O represents Input / Output. An I/O card provides the primary input and output connections for the CPU.

If you selected a motherboard that doesn't have onboard I/O, then you'll have to buy a separate I/O card. An I/O card is a low-cost add-in card that plugs into one of the add-on slots. In particular, we're interested in an IDE I/O card, not a SCSI I/O card. The IDE (for Integrated Drive Electronics) I/O card was originally designed to connect up to two low-cost hard drives to the computer.

Along the way, IDE became so popular that tape backup and CD-ROM drives were designed to use this inexpensive way to connect to the computer. Now the newer EIDE (Enhanced IDE) interface allows for faster data transfer and connections for up to four IDE devices (hard drives, tape drives, CD-ROM drives, etc.).

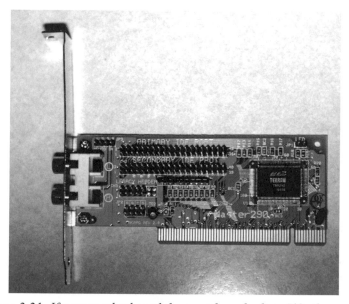

Figure 2.21 If your motherboard does not have built-in I/O, then you'll have to buy a separate I/O card similar to this one; it fits into a PCI slot.

When you're shopping for an I/O card, select one that supports the EIDE standard so that the devices that you connect to it can take advantage of the higher data transfer rate. Most EIDE I/O cards will support up to four fixed drives (hard drives and CD-ROM drives).

The I/O card also has connections for other types of input and output devices. Almost all I/O cards will support the following:

- ❖ Two floppy disk drives

- ❖ Two serial (communication) ports

- ❖ One parallel port

- ❖ One game port

Be sure to select an I/O card whose serial port is 16550 UART compatible. This ensures that the serial port is capable of communicating at higher data transfer rates without "losing" data, making it more reliable.

Keyboard

Many keyboards are available but they all fall into one of two categories: standard or ergonomic designs. The older style keyboard has 84-keys, and we doubt that you'll find these for sale any more. The extended AT-style keyboard has 101-keys including a numeric keypad and a second set of cursor keys. A new Windows 95 keyboard has two additional keys.

Figure 2.22 Standard and ergonomic style keyboards.

Ergonomic keyboards are shaped differently. They're designed to fit the contour of your hands and are said to be easier on your wrists and fingers. Figure 2.23 shows a standard and ergonomic style keyboard.

Consider an ergonomic style keyboard if you do a lot of typing. For example, the Microsoft Natural keyboard positions the hands slightly apart from one another. It takes a short time to get used to touch typing in this position, but it is quite comfortable to use.

The major suppliers of keyboards include:

- ❖ Acer
- ❖ Alps
- ❖ BTC
- ❖ Cherry
- ❖ Chicony
- ❖ Focus

❖ Fujitsu   ❖ Keytronix   ❖ Microsoft

❖ Mitsumi   ❖ Qtronix   ❖ Reveal

Mouse

We've lumped mice, trackballs and touchpads into the mouse category. These devices are all used to move the mouse pointer around on the screen.

One advantage trackballs and touchpads have over mice is that they don't require a large surface area in which to operate.

Here are a few of the popular "mouse" devices:

Figure 2.23 Mice, trackballs and touchpads let you move the mouse pointer around on the screen.

These devices are made by companies such as: Alps, Genius, Logitech, Microsoft and Mitsumi.

Floppy Drives

Floppy drives are for either 5.25" or 3.5" diskettes. Several years ago, almost all commercial software was distributed on 5.25" diskettes. Now, almost no software is made for the 5.25" format. Buy a 5.25" only if you have a need to transfer files between computers which still use these antiquated drives.

Some commercial software is still distributed on 3.5" diskettes, so you'll want a 3.5" floppy drive. These are still the easiest way to exchange small files between computers or friends. You can buy a brand name 3.5" drive such as Alps, Mitsumi, Panasonic, Sony and Teac for $15 to $30.

Hard Drives

There's a common saying that "you can never have too much hard disk space." It was true years ago and it's just as true today. Years ago, hard drive space was hardly affordable. But today you can hardly afford to do without gobs of space. Prices for IDE hard drives are so attractive that you shouldn't buy a hard drive with less than 2GB capacity. In fact, the price difference between a 2GB hard drive and a 4GB or 5GB drive is small, so we recommend that you select one with a larger capacity for your system.

Access time used to be a big consideration, but most drives deliver a track-to-track seek time of under 12 milliseconds, which is excellent. Don't worry too much about a two or three millisecond difference.

Select a drive from a major manufacturer:

- Fujitsu
- IBM
- Maxtor
- Microsoft
- NEC
- Quantum
- Samsung
- Seagate
- Toshiba
- Western Digital

CD-ROM Drives

You'll be able to find great bargains on 10x and slower CD-ROM drives. Resist the temptation and buy at least a 20x CD-ROM drive, or even 32x. Since you're building a fast Pentium computer system, you won't want to be slowed down by an older CD-ROM drive, especially if you plan to use your system for CD-ROM video applications.

CD-ROM drives can be connected to your computer in one of three ways: through the IDE interface, through a SCSI interface or through a proprietary interface. To minimize complexity, choose an IDE CD-ROM drive. We selected an IDE CD-ROM drive for the computer illustrated in this book. This eliminates the need for a separate add-in card to support the CD-ROM drive.

Again, select a drive from a major manufacturer:

❖ Acer	❖ Creative Labs	❖ Gold Star	❖ Toshiba
❖ Hitachi	❖ Mitsumi	❖ NEC	
❖ Pioneer	❖ Reveal	❖ Samsung	
❖ Sanyo	❖ Sony	❖ Teac	

Sound Cards

There are many varieties of sound cards. Almost all sound cards are "Sound Blaster" compatible, meaning programs written to work with Sound Blaster cards will also work with these sound cards.

We're not sound card experts, but we can definitely hear the difference in quality between an old 8-bit sound card and a newer wave table sound card. If you're on a tight budget and won't be using many audio applications, a 16-bit "Sound Blaster compatible" sound card will meet your needs. 32-bit wave table sound cards are more common today. If you will be regularly listening to or working with sounds, get a 64-bit card. We recommend that you look for a sound card that is Plug 'n' Play compatible, which greatly simplifies setup and configuration. For the computer in this book, we selected a 32-bit Plug 'n' Play sound card.

The major makers of sound cards are:

❖ Creative Labs	❖ Gravis	❖ Media Vision
❖ Reveal	❖ Turtle Beach	

Modems

Are you planning to access the Internet with a modem? Like other PC technologies, these have increased in speed while dropping in price. If you've ever downloaded an image with a slow modem, you know that speed is essential. A 56 KBPS (kilobauds per second) modem is easily the best choice. You may be able to find 33.6 or even 28.8 KBPS modems at very low prices.

All other things being equal, however, a 28.8 modem at its best will take twice as long to download information as a 56 KBPS modem. (It's also a good idea to ask your Internet service provider (ISP) about the highest connection speed it supports. A 56 KBPS modem will do you little good if your ISP only supports connections up to 33.6 KBPS.)

Some metropolitan areas now provide ISDN service. Using ISDN, you can connect to many service providers at speeds up to 128 KBPS! An ISDN modem is more expensive than a conventional modem, but if you are working from home or are going to be transferring large amounts of data, an investment in the more expensive ISDN modem will make your work more practical. Some ISDN modems are "combos"—they are backward compatible with conventional analog modems and also provide the faster digital technology of ISDN lines.

Well-known makers of modems include:

- Boca
- Cardinal
- Hayes
- Motorola
- Practical Peripherals
- Supra
- U.S. Robotics
- Zoom

Speakers

If you're familiar with hi-fi music speakers for your home stereo system, then you know that you can spend anywhere between $10 and $2000 for a speaker. It's almost the same for computer speakers. Computer speakers differ from conventional speakers in that they are self-amplified and magnetically shielded.

The inexpensive speakers are battery powered. We don't recommend them, since you'll surely spend a lot of money for batteries.

Most computer speakers are AC powered and have separate volume and tone controls.

You'll probably choose your speakers based on the maximum volume that you need from your multimedia programs and games.

Leading speaker manufacturers are:

- Altec-Lansing
- Bose
- Inland
- JBL
- Koss
- Labtec
- Reveal
- Sony
- Yamaha

Tape Backup

With today's large hard drive capacity, it's not practical to back up your valuable data to floppy diskette like it was a short time ago. Many of you don't acknowledge the need to back up your data. But there will come a time when you wish you had taken steps to safeguard all of the hours and energy that you spent to make your files, data and programs work perfectly on your system. One day—**POOF**—your hard drive will suddenly die, and you'll be left with no way to recover your files.

You can avoid this kind of disaster by investing in a backup system and making regularly scheduled backups.

Your choices for backup media have bloomed recently. Tape drives have been around for a while, and are still a reliable choice. These use cassettes (like overgrown audio cassettes) that are available in a variety of capacities. These are usually external devices.

Iomega produces the popular ZIP drives. ZIP disks are slightly larger than floppy disks, but can hold up to 100MB of data (that's about 70 times more than a floppy disk can hold). At around $100, these are a popular choice for backing up computers and for trading data with friends. ZIP drives are available internally and as external boxes.

Syquest makes similar backup units to ZIPs (also available as internal or external units). These are slightly more expensive, but they offer much more capacity. Each disk for the EZFlyer drive ($149) holds 230MB of data. Another model holds up to 1.5Gb.

Another option is the CD-Recordable and CD-ReWritable drives. These are CD drives that also allow you to create your own CDs, containing up to 650MB. These are still more expensive, but have the advantage of being compatible with virtually every computer.

Some of the more popular backup devices are made by:

- ❖ Colorado
- ❖ Iomega
- ❖ Syquest
- ❖ Teac
- ❖ Yamaha

Our Shopping List

During the writing of this book, we built two K6-2 computers from the ground up. We went shopping on two occasions and came back with the components listed below. We weren't aggressive shoppers—we didn't try to bargain the prices down.

Although we've listed the prices we paid, the prices you pay for similar items will vary widely depending on where you shop and the trend in computer prices. Currently, there's a downward trend. This means that you'll probably be able to build this same computer for less. But don't take our word for it. Go shopping, ask questions and expect straight answers.

Most of the components for System 1 were brand names. These components were packaged in normal retail shrink wrapped boxes with full manuals and installation diskettes.

For System 2, we tried to buy less expensive components. We bought most of these components at a local computer show. The components were packed "minimally"—usually in a sealed plastic bag with a plain, but clear instruction manual and installation diskettes.

We learned that by careful comparison shopping, we were able to find quality components at excellent prices. It takes some getting used to buying a hard drive that's wrapped in a plastic bag instead of a four-color, factory wrapped box. You'll have to decide if you need the security of full retail packaging or would rather save your hard-earned dollars buying "bulk" packaged components.

Table 2.24	
System 1	
AMD K6-2	$47
Asus P5A with Aladdin chipset	$100
2 32MB 8ns SDRAM DIMMs	$75
Matrox Millenium G400 16MB AGP	$133 boxed
Acer 40X E-IDE/ATAPI CD-ROM drive	$50 boxed
Maxstor 6.4 GB hard drive	$100
ATX mid-tower Case	$38 boxed
Panasonic 3.5" 1.44MB floppy drive	$25 boxed
Focus Windows ST keyboard	$15 boxed
Microsoft PS/2 style mouse	$25 boxed
Super Micro CPU cooling fan	$12 boxed
Creative Labs SB16 Plug n Play sound card	$24 boxed
Altec Lansing ALS-21	$25 boxed

Table 2.25	
System 2	
AMD K6-2 350	$47 installed
ASUS P5A with Aladdin chipset	$100 boxed
2 - 8MB 2 x 32 60ns 72-pin EDO SIMMS	$80
Trident PCI video card 1MB DRAM	$25 bagged
NewCom 32x ATAPI CD-ROM	$60 bagged
Fujitsu 4.3 GB hard drive	$95 bagged
AT Mini Tower case	$20 boxed
Mitsumi 3.5" 1.44MB floppy drive	$15 bagged
Mitsumi Windows 95 keyboard	$10 bagged
Generic PS/2 style mouse	$5 bagged
CPU cooling fan	$5 boxed
Creative Labs SB16 Plug n Play sound card	$25 bagged
Juster 200w stereo speakers	$8 bagged

3

Putting Your Computer Together

3 Putting Your Computer Together

Now that you've selected and bought all of your components, you're ready to assemble your computer system. We've laid out a step by step approach that we've successfully used to build and rebuild many different computers. No matter how excited or impatient you are about building your new computer, please follow all of the steps in the order in which we've presented them. We don't want you to make a mistake that ends up "frying" one of the components.

WARNING

Electrical energy is dangerous. You should know that a computer is an electrical appliance. As such, you must take precautions against electrical shock. Always unplug the computer's power supply from the power outlet before you attempt to add, move or remove a component.

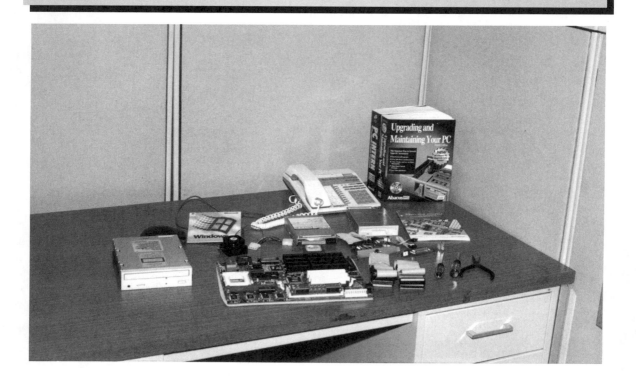

STEP

1

Prepare a work area

It's easier said than done, but make the effort to clear a flat, work area about six feet by four feet in size so you can assemble your PC without falling over yourself.

An oversized card table or an unused workbench or desk works well. The work surface should be clean. If the work surface cannot be washed, spread clean, white paper over the area. We don't recommend using newspaper because it's hard to find small parts when they drop on news articles and pictures.

The work area should be well lighted; it's usually dark when you're working inside a computer case and the extra light will make assembling your PC much easier. Stay away from drafty areas since small parts are likely to be blown away and lost.

Figure 3.1 A clear well-lighted work area speeds the assembly.

STEP 2 — Gather your tools

Contrary to what you might think, you don't need very many tools to assemble a computer. Most of you will have the necessary tools already. Here's what you'll need:

* Phillips Screwdriver #1 head

* Screwdriver 1/8" blade

* Nutdriver 3/8"

* Long-nose pliers

* Several small paper cups (the small bathroom size Dixie cups are great) for holding small screws and parts

* Large mouse pad or small hand towel on which to place the motherboard

* A pen and a pad of paper to take notes

* Hammer (to be used only when you can't get the computer to work—JUST KIDDING!)

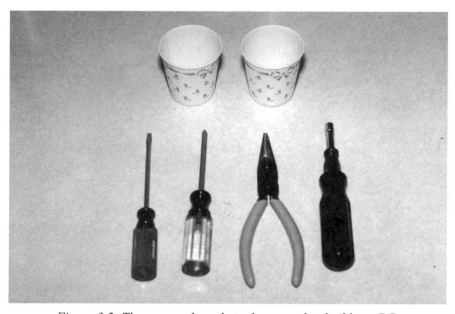

Figure 3.2 These were the only tools we used to build our PC.

If the only Phillips head screwdriver you own is too big or too small, then STOP. Go to a hardware store and buy one that's the correct size. You risk damaging the components or stripping the screw heads by using the wrong tool. A new tool costs only a few dollars. Compare this small expense to the amount of money that you've invested in your new computer.

STEP 3 Prepare the case

Remove the case from its packaging and place it upright on your work surface with the back of the case facing you. Remove the case's cover. Usually five or six hex head screws are used to attach the cover to the frame. Unscrew these and place them in a small paper cup. Label the cup so that you'll know where the screws came from. You can set the cover aside and away from the work area for now. You won't need the cover for a while.

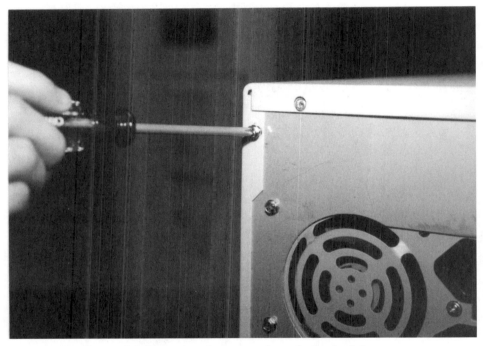

Figure 3.3 Removing the screws from the back of the case.

Now lay the case horizontally with the motherboard chassis closest to the work surface and the power supply closest to you, as in Figure 3.4.

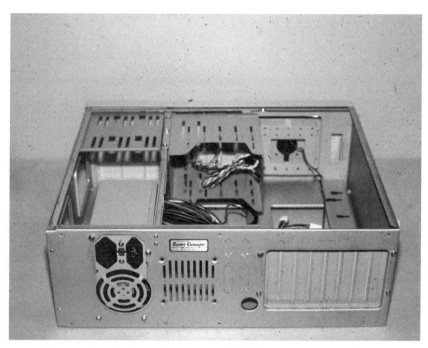

Figure 3.4   Position the case with the back facing toward you.

Some cases, especially tower models, have a removable cage in which you can mount some of the storage devices: floppies, hard drives, CD-ROMs, tape backup drives, etc. After you remove the cage by unscrewing a few hex head screws as in Figure 3.5, you'll have a less obstructed work area inside the case.

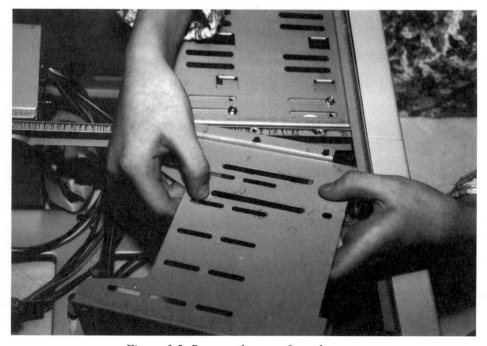

Figure 3.5   Remove the cage from the case.

After the cage is removed, the entire chassis on bottom of the case is exposed, as in Figure 3.6. This makes is much easier for you to mount the motherboard in the case.

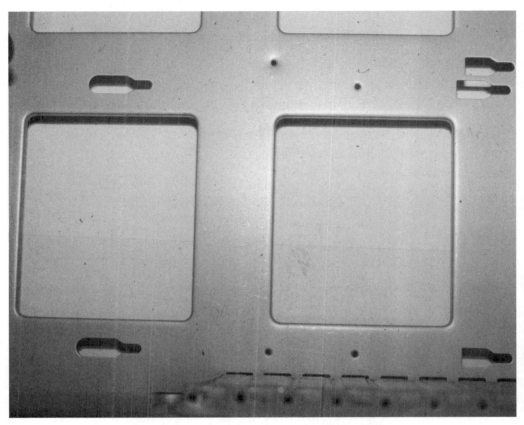

Figure 3.6 Plastic standoffs are later inserted into the oblong cutouts in the chassis to mount the motherboard to the case.

Note the oblong cutouts in the chassis. In a few minutes, you'll see how the plastic standoffs are inserted in these cutouts to mount the motherboard to the case (See Step 9).

STEP
4

Rid yourself of electrostatic energy

Electrostatic energy (we used to call it static electricity) is capable of damaging computer circuits in some of the components. To prevent damaging them, you'll need to discharge yourself of this deadly "disease" before handling the components.

A simple way to do this is to ground yourself. When your power supply is plugged into a three-prong wall outlet, the computer case is also grounded. To discharge yourself of the electrostatic energy, touch the metal computer case.

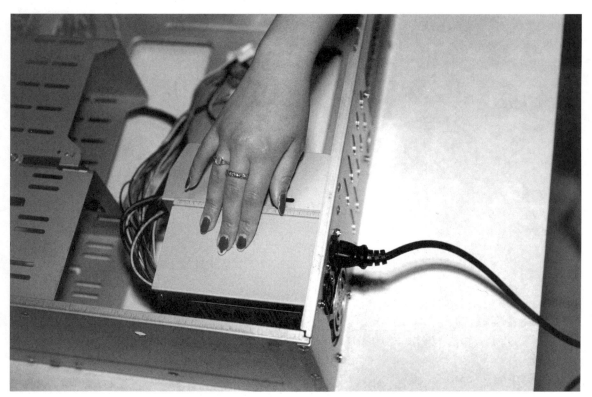

Figure 3.7 You can discharge yourself of electrostatic energy by grounding yourself to the case.

Another way to discharge yourself of electrostatic energy is to wear a wrist strap. This device is like a watch with a leash. The leash is connected to a ground and the other end wraps around your wrist. You're always grounded by wearing the wrist strap.

STEP 5 — Configure the motherboard

The next step is to *configure* or set up the motherboard. You'll now have to <u>carefully read the user's manual</u> for your motherboard. You'll have to find the instructions for setting any DIP switches and/or jumpers for the computer that you are about to build. Before you get started, we'll cover a few basics that will be helpful.

DIP switches are usually found in sets of from two to eight miniature light switches on a small plastic base which is soldered to the top of the motherboard. The individual switches are numbered and the label on the plastic base indicates whether a given switch is on or off. To turn a switch on, use a ball-point pen to move the switch in the **ON** direction. To turn a switch off, move the switch **opposite the ON** direction. A row of DIP switches on a motherboard looks like this:

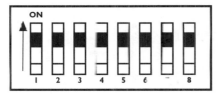

Figure 3.8 Example of a DIP switch that might be found on a motherboard.

A jumper is another kind of switch. You'll notice that there are several metal pins sticking up from the surface of the motherboard. The pins are labeled JP1 or J10, for example. A jumper cap is a small metal connector surrounded by insulated plastic (most jumper caps are black in color). When you put the jumper cap on two of the pins, you *close* or *turn on* the switch. If you don't put a jumper cap on the pins, then the switch is *open* or *turned off*. In some cases the pins on the motherboard are paired and labeled 1 and 2; in other cases, there may be three pins labeled 1, 2 and 3. You may be asked to select one option by jumpering pins 1 and 2 or other option by jumpering pins 2 and 3.

In Figure 3.9, the setting is made by jumpering pins 2 and 3.

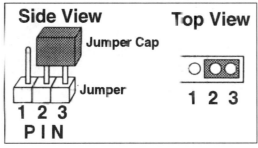

Figure 3.9 A typical jumper on a motherboard.

In this book we also refer to a *connector*. In one instance, a connector may refer to a set of pins on the motherboard (usually from 2 to 40 pins). A connector may also refer to the black plastic plug at the end of a set of wires or cable which is attached to the pins.

For the K6-2 computer that we're building in this book, we are going configure the motherboard in the following illustration:

Figure 3.10 This Pentium motherboard has a Triton II chipset and built-in I/O board.

Here's a schematic diagram of the same motherboard so you can more easily pick out the important landmarks. The labels refer to the jumpers and connectors as they are identified in the Motherboard User's Guide.

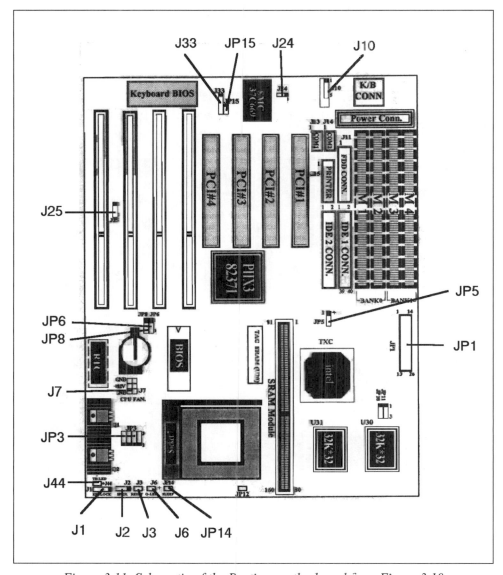

Figure 3.11 Schematic of the Pentium motherboard from Figure 3.10.

Before you handle the motherboard, first rid yourself of electrostatic energy.

Place the motherboard on a soft padded surface. A large mouse mat or a terrycloth hand towel will work well. Our motherboard was packed with a white foam pad which is good for preventing any damage to the work surface (the bottom of the motherboard has sharp edges) or to the motherboard itself.

We've reproduced several pages of the user's guide so that you can see what is required to configure this particular motherboard. Unfortunately, most motherboard user's guides are poorly written. The user's guide for this motherboard is no exception. The writer is inconsistent in the way that he labels the jumpers and connectors (he incorrectly uses the notation J and JP which normally signifies connector and jumper respectively). Furthermore, the writer's choice of words, grammar and sentence structure make it more difficult for us to interpret what he's trying to say.

Figure 3.12 is a page from the user's guide that identifies the arrangement of connectors. Since there are no switches or jumpers listed on this page, we do not have to set any. We'll use the information on this page again later when completing the motherboard installation.

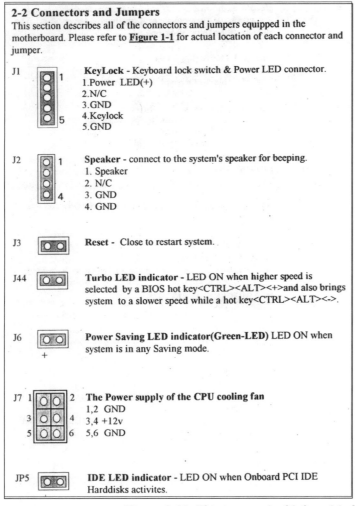

	Interpretation
J1	This is a connector, not a switch. No setting is required
J2	This is a connector, not a switch. No setting is required
J3	This is a connector, not a switch. No setting is required
J44	This is a connector, not a switch. No setting is required
J6	This is a connector, not a switch. No setting is required
J7	This is a connector, not a switch. No setting is required
JP5	This is a connector, not a switch. No setting is required

Figure 3.12 This is page 1 of 3 from Motherboard User's Guide.

Figure 3.13 is a second page of the user's guide that describes the use of several jumpers. Since we used the factory default settings, we didn't have to change any of the settings listed on this page.

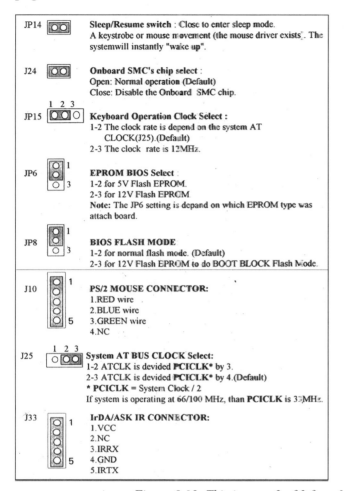

	Interpretation
JP14	Although it is described as a switch, it's actually a connector so no setting is required
J24	The SMC chip select handles the onboard I/O. We'll use the default setting by leaving the jumper OPEN
JP5	We'll use the default setting by leaving pins 1 and 2 jumpered.
JP6	We'll use the default setting by leaving pins 2 and 3 jumpered.
JP8	We'll use the default setting by leaving pins 1 and 2 jumpered.
J10	This is a connector. No setting is required
J25	We'll use the default setting by leaving pins 2 and 3 jumpered.
J33	This is a connector. No setting is required

Figure 3.13 This is page 2 of 3 from Motherboard User's Guide.

JP1:CPU Clock Rate Select.

	Pentium® Processor	Cyrix 6x86 Processor	
1-14	50/75MHz		
2-15	60/90MHz		
3-16	66/100MHz		(Default)
4-17	60/120MHz	6x86-P150+(120MHz)	
5-18	66/133MHz	6x86-P166+(133MHz)	
6-19	60/150MHz		
7-20	66/166MHz		
8-21	60/180MHz		
9-22	66/200MHz		
10-23		6x86-P120+(100MHz)	
11-24			
12-25			
13-26			

JP3

CPU Install:
1-2:   for Intel Pentium® Processor (P54C/P54CS/
        P54CT/P54CTB) and Cyrix 6x86(Note)
2-3:   Intel Pentium® Processor P55C.

Interpretation	
JP	We're building a PC with a Pentium 166 MHz CPU. According to the manual, we have to jumper pins 7 and 20. Depending on the speed of the CPU that you're installing on the motherboard, you would jumper the corresponding pins. See Figure 3.14 for detailed view.
JP	We'll use the default setting where all sets of pin 1 and 2 are jumpered since we're using one of the P54 series of Intel processors.

Figure 3.14   This is page 3 of 3 from Motherboard User's Guide.

Figure 3.15   Jumpering pins 7 and 20 to configure the motherboard for a 166MHz CPU.

As you can see, there weren't very many jumpers or switches that we needed to set for this particular motherboard. Still, you'll have to read the user's manual for your particular motherboard in detail. If you have questions about the settings, ask the salesperson or technician from whom you bought the motherboard. They have a lot of experience building PCs and should be quite familiar with the specific settings for the motherboards they sell.

STEP 6

Install the CPU on the motherboard

This is an easy step. All motherboards for the K6-2 CPU have a ZIF socket. ZIF stands for Zero Insertion Force and as its name suggests, you don't have to apply any pressure to insert the CPU into the socket.

Unlatch the small plastic or metal arm on the side of the ZIF socket and lift the arm until it is standing upright. Notice that there is a small notch on one of the four corners of your K6-2 CPU. Turn the CPU upside down and you'll see three gold pins that run diagonally to the corner. On the ZIF socket, you'll also see three small holes that run diagonally to the corner. This indicates the alignment of the CPU and

> **Special Tip**
>
> Discharge yourself of any electrostatic energy before you handle the CPU.

socket. You'll only be able to insert the CPU into the socket by aligning the diagonal pins and holes. Carefully insert the CPU into the socket making sure that the CPU is fully seated. You do not have to push the CPU into the socket as it will easily drop into place on its own. If it doesn't, wiggle the arm a bit. See Figures 3 16, 3.17 and 3.18.

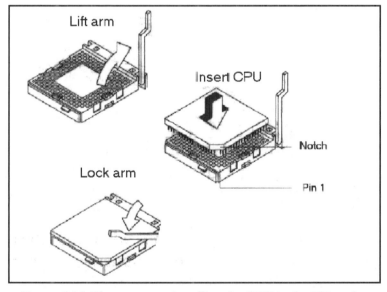

Figure 3.16 Three steps to installing the CPU in the ZIF socket.

Figure 3.17 Gently place the CPU into the socket...

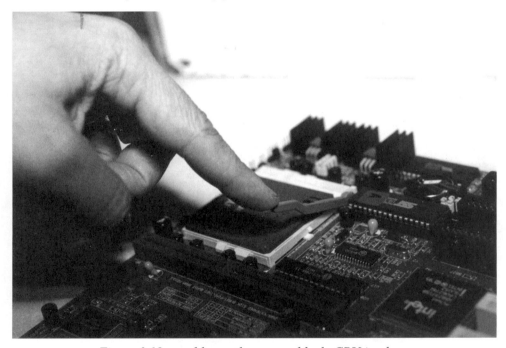

Figure 3.18 ...and lower the arm and lock CPU in place.

When the CPU is properly seated in the ZIF socket, lower the arm fully and latch it so that the CPU is locked into place.

STEP 7 · Install the cache memory on the motherboard

Some motherboards have cache memory already installed. Figure 3.19 shows a motherboard that was manufactured with 256K of pipeline burst cache onboard.

Figure 3.19   Motherboard with onboard cache.

Your motherboard may also have onboard cache memory and/or may have one or more sockets for adding cache memory. The cache memory may be individual static RAM chips or COAST modules.

WARNING

Before you handle the cache memory chips or module, make sure that you've discharged yourself of any electrostatic energy.

If your motherboard uses the individual static RAM chips, then you'll have to install them by aligning the notched corner of the static RAM chip with the notch indicator on the socket and gently pushing the chip into its socket. Be careful not to bend the delicate pins. See Figure 3.20.

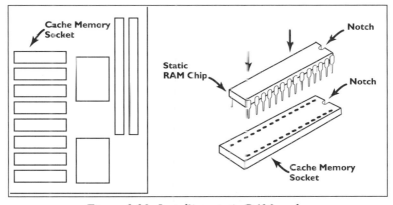

Figure 3.20 Installing static RAM cache.

In addition to the onboard cache, this particular motherboard has a socket which accepts a pipeline burst cache (COAST) module. Installing a COAST module, increases the amount of cache memory on this motherboard from 256K to 512K. If you've purchased a COAST module, you can simply plug it into the motherboard. You can only insert the COAST module into its socket in one direction, so there's no chance of putting it in backwards. (See Figure 3.21.)

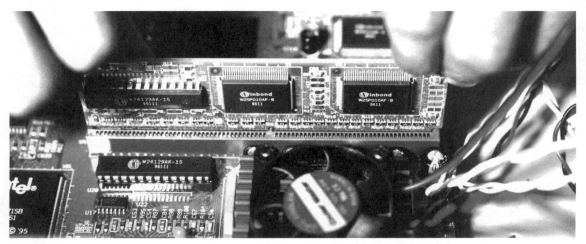

Figure 3.21 Installing a COAST pipeline burst cache module.

STEP 8 Install memory on the motherboard

Installing main memory is also easy. Memory is supplied on 72-pin SIMM modules. This motherboard can accept up to four SIMM modules, one in each of the four white sockets in the upper right hand corner of Figure 3.10.

The four sockets are arranged as two banks of two sockets each. In our Motherboard User's Guide, a schematic of the sockets indicated that one is labeled Bank 0 and the other Bank 1. If you are installing only two SIMMs, these must be installed in Bank 0. At a later time, if you want to install two more SIMMs, they'll be installed in Bank 1. Make sure that you know which sockets are Bank 0 and which are Bank 1 as in the following figure:

Figure 3.22 Two SIMM sockets each make up Bank 0 and Bank 1.

Discharge yourself of electrostatic energy before touching any of the SIMM modules.

Pick up one of the SIMM modules. Find the small holes on each side of the module. Beneath one of the holes you'll see a notch. This notch is designed to prevent you from inserting the SIMM module into a socket backwards. Examine the SIMM socket and note which direction you'll have to insert the SIMM module so that the notch will clear the plastic tab. With the metal fingers side down, carefully insert the SIMM module into a socket in Bank 0 in the noted direction. The module is inserted into the socket at a 30 degree angle from vertical. The metal fingers will line up perfectly with the fingers in the socket. If you happen to insert the SIMM backwards, the fingers will not align correctly and the notch will not clear the plastic tab. The holes in the SIMM will align with the pegs on the socket and the metal clips on the sockets will click to indicate that the SIMMs are locked in place. See Figure 3.23 and Figure 3.24.

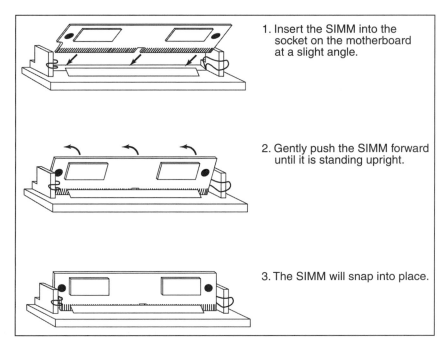

Figure 3.23 Installing memory on the motherboard.

This is what it looks like from a different angle:

*Figure 3.24 This is a view from the front side of the figure
on the top of the page as we install the SIMM into a socket.*

Remember that SIMM modules must be installed in pairs and that both SIMM modules in the same bank must have the same memory capacity. So for example, 32MB of memory is added to a computer system by installing two 16MB SIMMs into one of the banks. Alternatively, you can install four 8MB SIMMs into both of the banks.

You may have selected DIMM memory instead of SIMMs (see Chapter Two), in which case the installation is even easier. DIMMs do not need to be installed in pairs, though you may have several slots available for these modules. If so, install memory in bank zero first. Each DIMM has two notches along the bottom edge. These prevent you from installing the modules in the wrong direction. To install the DIMM, line up the notches with the slot in the board and insert the DIMM straight down. As you insert the DIMM, the tabs on the sides of the slot will move into position. (Push down on these tabs to remove the DIMM.)

Mount the motherboard in the case

Your case includes a small box or plastic bag containing the mounting hardware.

Figure 3.25 A packet containing the hardware for mounting the motherboard to the case.

Among the mounting hardware are screws of various sizes and *standoffs*. Here's a picture of several types of standoffs so that you'll be able to identify them.

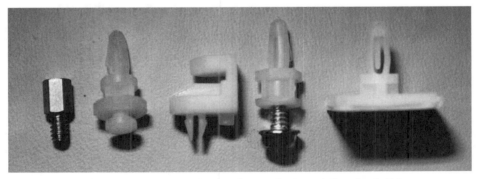

Figure 3.26 Standoffs– from left to right Brass, Standard, Edge,
Screw down, and Adhesive backed.
(Courtesy of Skyline Computers, Brookfield, IL)

As you can see, there are different styles of standoffs. Usually, only the brass, standard and edge standoffs are included with the hardware packet.

A standoff is used to attach the motherboard to the case. At the same time, the standoff holds the motherboard a safe distance away from the metal chassis to prevent unwanted connections from shorting out.

Figure 3.27 Examples of brass standoffs and machine mounting screws.

The brass standoffs in Figure 3.27 are screwed directly into the case. When secured to the brass standoff with a machine screw, the motherboard is grounded to the case.

The trick in mounting the motherboard is to line up the holes in the chassis with the holes in the motherboard. An easy way to do this is to take a large piece of paper, scotch tape it to the bottom of the chassis and carefully trace the outline of the cutouts and small screw holes with a felt marker. Note the location of the keyboard connector cutout on the back side of the case's frame on the paper template. Untape the paper from the chassis. It should look similar to Figure 3.28.

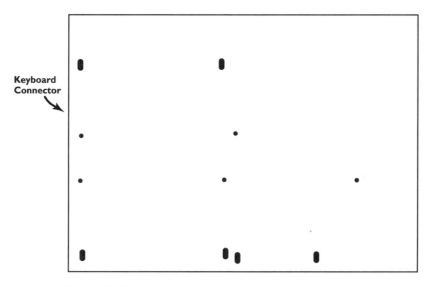

*Figure 3.28 This paper template indicates the position
of the cutouts and screw holes on the chassis.*

Now place the motherboard over the paper template so that the keyboard connector is in the same relative position as indicated on the paper template as in Figure 3.29. Move the motherboard until its holes are aligned with the holes that you traced on the template. Not all of the holes will be lined up. Note those holes that <u>are</u> lined up. Draw an "X" on the paper template to mark the holes that are lined up exactly. These X's are the points at which you will soon attach the motherboard to the chassis. For a secure installation, you'll want to attach the motherboard to the chassis at a minimum of six or seven points.

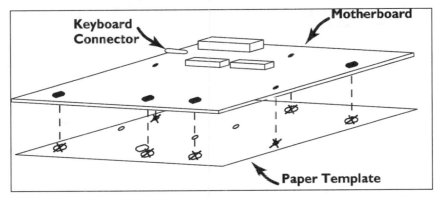

Figure 3.29 Identify the holes on the motherboard which are aligned with the holes in the case.

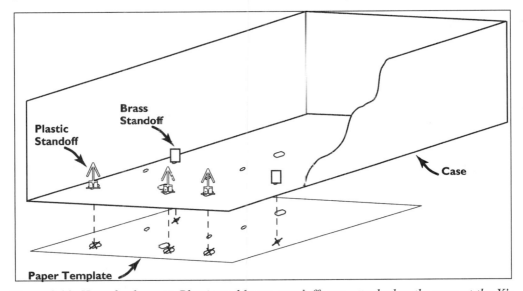

Figure 3.30 X marks the spot. Plastic and brass standoffs are attached to the case at the X's.

Now place the paper template beneath the case once again (as in Figure 3.30). The areas marked with an "X" on the paper template indicate the points at which the plastic and metal standoffs are attached to the case. Now you'll insert the plastic and metal standoffs in cutouts and holes in the case corresponding to the "X" on the paper template.

To attach a plastic standoff to the chassis, insert the short end into the larger end of the oblong cutout and slide it towards the smaller end. Make sure that the sides of the metal opening slide into the plastic groove. See Figure 3.31.

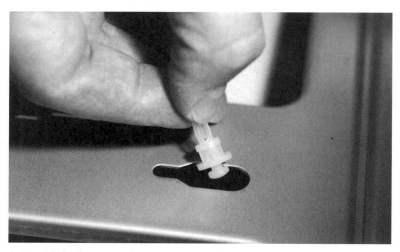

Figure 3.31   Slide the standard plastic standoff into the oblong cutout in the chassis.

To attach a metal standoff, simply screw it into the desired chassis holes. The metal standoffs also serve to ground the motherboard to the case.

Attach the desired number of standoffs to the case. Gently lower motherboard into the case and align the holes over the standoffs. First secure the motherboard to the brass standoffs as in the following figure. Screw the motherboard to each of the brass standoffs with the mounting screws from your accessory package. As you're doing this, you'll see the heads of the plastic standoffs peeking through the holes in the motherboard as in Figure 3.32. When all of the screws have been secured, gently press the motherboard at a point close to each of the plastic standoffs. The top of the plastic standard standoffs will pop through the holes in the motherboard and open up (like an umbrella) to hold the motherboard in place Tighten the screws again. You've just completed the physical mounting.

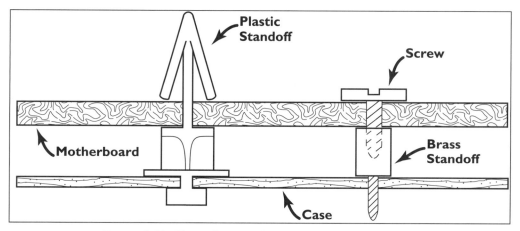

Figure 3.32 This side view shows you how the plastic and brass standoffs are used to mount the motherboard to the chassis.

Now check to make sure that there are no surface areas on the bottom of the motherboard that are touching the metal case. If there are, remove the motherboard and reinstall it. Otherwise, the motherboard will short circuit on the case and become damaged. When you're done, the bottom of the case will look similar to Figure 3.33:

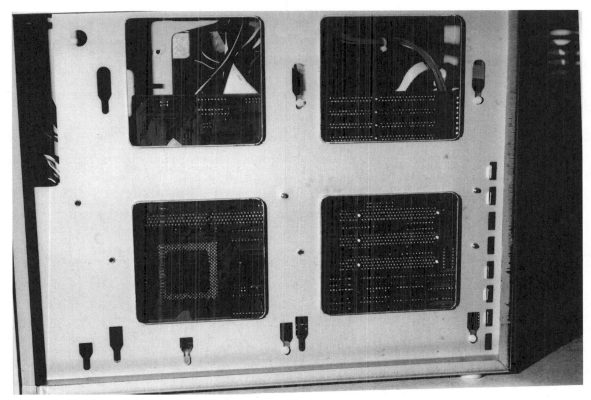

*Figure 3.33 A bottom view of the chassis after the motherboard
has been mounted to the case using the plastic and brass standoffs.*

If You Have Trouble

Sometimes the holes in the motherboard just will not line up with the cutouts and screw holes on the chassis.

If this happens, you can purchase either screw down standoffs or adhesive backed standoffs. Either of these standoffs can be placed anywhere on the chassis. For screw down standoffs, you'll have to drill a hole in the desired position on the chassis. For the adhesive backed standoffs, you can remove the protective backing and press the standoff in the desired position.

Connect the power supply to the motherboard

There are usually six or seven sets of wires (harnesses) leading from the power supply. Locate the two connectors. They have six wires each. These connectors are usually labeled "P8" and "P9." They supply power to the motherboard.

Figure 3.34 shows a power supply that we removed from its case so you could see the connectors more easily.

Figure 3.34 The two sets of wires in the left foreground labeled P8 and P9 have six wires each. These connect to the motherboard.

The connectors are designed to attach to the motherboard in only one direction. If the connector does not attach easily, then it's probably on backwards. The ribbed side of the P8 and P9 connectors should face the power supply connector on the motherboard. Attach both 6-pin connectors (P8 and P9) to the 12-pin connector on the motherboard so that the four black wires are located in the middle of the 12-pin connector. **Check and double-check** to make sure that they're correctly connected so that you won't fry your motherboard.

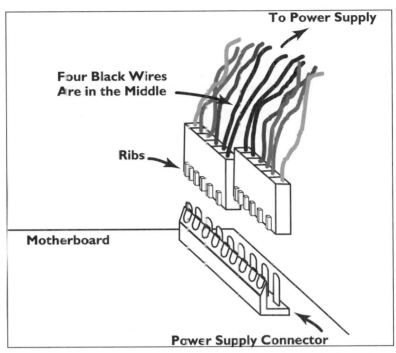

Figure 3.35 Connecting the power supply to the motherboard.

STEP

11

Connect the other case wires to the motherboard

Inside the case you'll find several twisted sets of wires leading out from the back of the front panel. The small connectors at the end of the wires are usually clearly labeled to identify their function. These are connected to various pins on the motherboard.

You'll have to consult the motherboard user's manual again to determine the location of the pins to which you'll attach the connectors.

Special Tip

Keep in mind that these connections will likely be different for your case and motherboard. We show you the connections for the motherboard in this example so you can better understand how we were able to determine which connections to make.

❖ **J1 KeyLock**

Our case has two separate connectors that attach to the pins on connector J1 of this motherboard:

1. On our case, the green and white wires are for the power LED. This is attached to pins 1, 2 and 3 of J1.

2. On our case, one of two sets of red and black wires is for the keylock. The other set of red and black wires is for the speaker. Identify the set of wires leading from the keylock and attach this connector to pins 4 and 5 of J1.

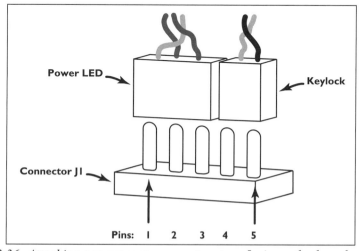

Figure 3.36 Attaching two separate connectors to a 5-pin motherboard connector.

❖ **J2 Speaker**

On our case, the second set of black and red wires lead from the speaker. Identify these and attach the connector to pins 1 through 4 of J2.

❖ **J3 Reset**

On our case, the blue and white wires are for the reset switch. Attach the connector to pins 1 and 2 of J3.

❖ **J44 Turbo LED indicator**

On our case, the yellow and white wires are for the turbo LED indicator. Attach the connector to pins 1 and 2 of J44.

❖ **JP5 IDE LED indicator**

On our case, the red and white wires are for the HDD LED. HDD is an abbreviation for <u>H</u>ard <u>D</u>isk <u>D</u>rive, which is an IDE device. Attach this connector to pins 1 and 2 of JP5.

Figure 3.37 Most of the "other" connectors are on the edge of the motherboard closest to the front on the case.

Because the Pentium generates heat, you'll have to install a CPU cooling fan to prevent it from overheating and damaging itself.

A CPU cooling fan includes a metal heat sink and the fan housing. Before installing the cooling fan, first make sure the top of the CPU is clean. If not, gently wipe the top ceramic surface with a cloth. To work properly, the heat sink has to make good contact with the top surface of the CPU. Fit the heat sink carefully over the top of the CPU. Next clip the fan housing over both the heat sink and the CPU making sure that it is securely fastened to the edge of the ZIF socket. Most fan housings clasp over the edge of the socket.

Figure 3.38 Installing the CPU cooling fan.

Plug the cooling fan cable into a power supply connector. Make sure that the other wires or cables will not obstruct the airflow of the fan.

Pause: Tips For Installing Add-on Cards

Before we continue, we want to take a short break to explain how to install add-on cards in the expansion slots on the motherboard. In some computer cases, the expansion slot covers are stamped into the case's back panel. To remove a slot cover, carefully bend it back and forth until the bottom "tears" away from the panel. As you do this, be careful not to damage any of the tiny components on the motherboard. Figure 3.39 below shows how you remove one of the expansion slot covers.

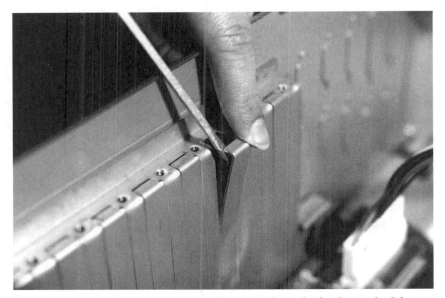

Figure 3.39   Removing an expansion slot cover from the back panel of the case.

In other computer cases, the expansion slot covers are screwed into the back panel. To remove a slot cover, unscrew the screw holding the cover in place.

Tips

Here are tips to follow when installing any card into an expansion slot:

❖ Carefully insert the edge of the card into the slot.
❖ Rock the board back and forth slightly from front to back until it seats securely in the slot and the metal fingers are making positive contact.
❖ Check that no part of the card is pressing on any of the delicate motherboard components underneath.
❖ Verify that the metal plate on the card aligns perfectly with the back of the case.
❖ Screw the metal plate into the case to complete the physical installation.

Now we're ready to connect the peripherals. This motherboard has built-in onboard I/O. You may have bought a separate I/O card. If so, you can insert it into one of the ISA slots on the motherboard and secure it with a screw to the back of the case. In subsequent steps, when we refer to "connectors on the motherboard," you should substitute "connectors on the I/O board."

If you've removed the cage, you can now reinstall it since the motherboard is securely seated in the case.

Here are the cables that attach the peripherals to the motherboard:

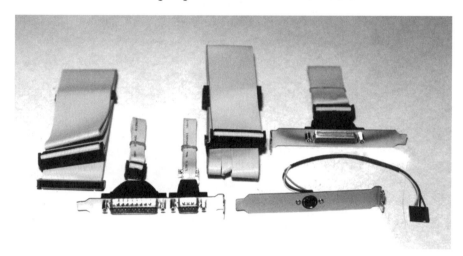

*Figure 3.40 Here's all the connecting cables that you'll use
to attach peripherals to the motherboard.*

STEP 13 Install the floppy drive

The front panel of your case has several removable plastic or metal plates covering the drive bays. The narrow plates cover the bays for 3.5" drives while the wider plates cover the bays for 5.25" drives.

These plates can be removed from the front panel by gently popping them out from the front panel. Remove one of the plates for your 3.5" floppy drive (as in Figure 3.41).

Next slide the floppy drive into one of the 3.5 ' bays so that the front of the drive is flush with the front, as in Figure 3.42. Then secure the drive to the case with at least four screws. You may have to flip the case on its other side to secure both sides of the drive to the mounting brackets.

A 34-wire ribbon cable is used to connect the floppy drive to the motherboard (or I/O card). In Figure 3.43, you can see that one end of the cable connects to the floppy controller on either the motherboard or a separate I/O board.

The other end has two connectors for the A drive. One of these is for a floppy drive that has an edge connector and the other is for a floppy drive that has a 34-pin connector. See Figure 3.44.

In the middle are two connectors for the B drive. Again, one is for an edge connector and the other for a 34-pin connector.

Figure 3.41 (top right) Remove the face plate from the front cover of the case.

Figure 3.42 (bottom right) Slide the floppy drive into the case from the front.

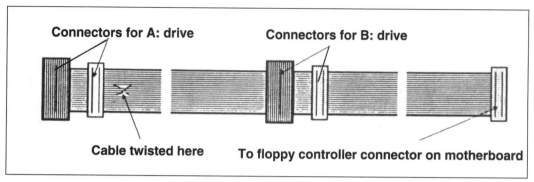

Figure 3.43 A 34-wire ribbon cable connects floppy drive to the motherboard or I/O board.

Most likely, your floppy drive will have a 34-pin connector since the edge connectors are ancient. In any case, plug either the 34-pin connector or the edge connector into the back of the floppy drive. The edge connector on the ribbon is "keyed" so it will fit onto the floppy drive in only one direction. Then plug one of the power supply connectors into the back of the floppy drive as in Figure 3.45.

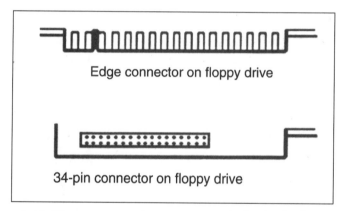

Figure 3.44 The two types of connectors on the back of a floppy drive.

Along the length of the cable is a color line which indicates pin 1 on the connector. Plug the 34-pin connector into the floppy controller port on the motherboard (or separate I/O board) making sure that pin 1 of the connector matches pin 1 on the board. See Figure 3.46.

Figure 3.45 Plug the power supply cable and the 34-pin connector (A-drive) into the floppy drive.

Figure 3.46 Plug the 34-pin ribbon cable from the floppy drive to the motherboard (or separate I/O card).

STEP 14   Install the IDE hard drive

Since the hard drive will be totally enclosed within the case, you won't have to remove a plastic or metal plate from the case's front panel to install your hard drive. Slide the hard drive into one of the bays so that the connectors on the drive are accessible. Secure the hard drive to the case with four screws.

A 40-wire ribbon cable is used to connect the hard drive to the motherboard (or I/O card). The ribbon cable has three 40-pin connectors—one at each end and a third about one-third of the way towards one end as in Figure 3.47.

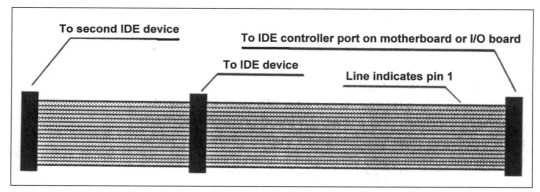

Figure 3.47 A 40-wire ribbon cable connects IDE devices to the motherboard or I/O board.

Plug the other end of the cable into the connector on the hard drive. Again, make certain that pin 1 on the cable matches pin 1 of the hard drive. Plug one of the power supply connectors into the hard drive as in Figure 3.48.

A color line (usually red) along the length of the cable ribbon indicates pin 1, similar to the 34-pin floppy cable. Plug one end of the 40-pin connectors into the primary IDE controller connector on the motherboard (or separate I/O board) making sure that pin 1 of the connector matches pin 1 on the board (as in Figure 3.49).

Figure 3.48 Plug the 40-pin connector and the power supply connector into the back of the hard drive.

Figure 3.49 Plug the 40-pin connector into the motherboard (or separate I/O card).

STEP 15 Install the IDE CD-ROM drive

Remove one of the plastic or metal plates from the front panel that covers a 5.25" bay. Regardless of the make of an IDE CD-ROM drive, they are configured similarly. To be absolutely sure, you'll want to refer to the CD-ROM drive installation manual. Our explanation is a general one, but it should be similar to that from your installation manual.

An IDE device—hard drive or CD-ROM drive—is set as a master device or a slave device by setting a jumper on the rear of the drive. If the IDE controller port already has one device attached (our computer already has the hard drive connected), then that device (the hard drive) is the master and the second device (the CD-ROM) is the slave. Therefore you set the jumper on the CD-ROM drive which makes it a slave. This is usually the default setting from the factory.

After you set the jumper, slide the CD-ROM drive into the bay so that the front of the CD-ROM drive is flush with the front. Secure the CD-ROM drive to the case with four screws. Locate the middle 40-pin connector on the ribbon cable and plug it into the back of the CD-ROM drive as you align pin 1 of the connector to pin 1 of the CD-ROM drive. Plug a 4-wire power cable into the power connector on the CD-ROM drive. See Figure 3.50.

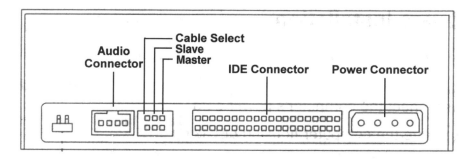

Figure 3.50 The back of a typical IDE CD-ROM drive.

Alternative:

You can also connect the CD-ROM to the secondary IDE controller port. If no other devices are connected to the secondary IDE controller, then you would set the jumper on the CD-ROM drive which makes it a master. Some manufacturers recommend that you use this setup so the performance of a hard drive sharing the same cable is not adversely affected by the slower CD-ROM transfer rate. If you choose this method, you must use a second 40-pin ribbon cable and plug one connector into the secondary IDE port and the other end into the CD-ROM drive.

In order to hear audio through your sound card, you'll have to connect the CD-ROM drive to the sound card with an audio cable. One end of the cable attaches to the rear of the CD-ROM drive and the other plugs into the sound card.

STEP 16 — Install the video display card

This motherboard has four PCI slots (white) and four ISA/EISA slots (brown). Since we have selected a PCI video display card, we'll insert the card into one of the PCI slots. Secure the card to the back of the case with a screw.

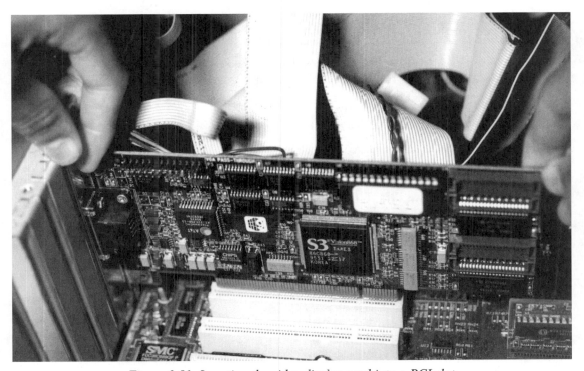

Figure 3.51 Inserting the video display card into a PCI slot.

Like most others, you do not have to change any settings on this video display card.

STEP 17   Install sound card

Because we've selected a Plug 'n' Play sound card, there aren't any jumpers or switches that we have to set on this card.

If you are installing a conventional sound card (not Plug 'n Play), then you may have to set jumpers or switches so that the operation of the sound card does not interfere with the operation of any other devices connected to the computer. Since there are so many different sound cards, we can't tell you how to configure any particular sound card, but the default settings are often a good place to start. Creative Labs Sound Blaster and compatible cards usually have a default of I/O port address 220, IRQ 5, DMA 1 which usually work well.

Insert the sound card into one of the ISA slots. Secure the card to back of the case with a screw. Plug the speakers into the sound card.

Refer to the sound card installation manual to locate the CD audio connector. Plug the audio cable from the CD-ROM into the CD audio connector on the sound card.

STEP 18 — Connect the mouse port to the motherboard

This motherboard has a connector for a PS/2-style mouse port.

The PS/2 style connector for the mouse is mounted onto a metal expansion slot cover. A narrow ribbon cable (or wire harness) runs between this connector and the motherboard.

Plug the six-pin connector into the appropriate connector on the motherboard (for our motherboard it's J10), making sure that pin 1 on the motherboard corresponds to pin 1 on the connector (colored line indicates pin 1). Next mount the expansion slot cover with the mouse port onto the back panel of the case (as in Figure 3.52).

Finally, plug the mouse into the mouse port (as in Figure 3.53).

Figure 3.52 Securing the mouse port to the case.

Figure 3.53 Plug the mouse in the PS/2 mouse port.

STEP 19 **Connect the serial ports to motherboard**

This motherboard has built in I/O capabilities. If you're using a separate I/O card, then you'll also have these same I/O capabilities.

Figure 3.54   Securing a 9-pin serial port connector to the back of the case.

Part of these capabilities include two serial communication ports. Both of the serial ports mount on the back panel of the case. There are usually removable knockouts on the back panel for various connectors. The connectors are either the smaller 9-pin connector or the larger 25-pin connector. Both are male gender. Remove one or both of the knockouts for the desired connector size.

Mount the metal connector(s) to the case with two hex screws, as in Figure 3.54. A flat ribbon runs between this connector and attaches to the motherboard (or separate I/O board) with a 10-pin plastic connector. The motherboard connectors are usually clearly labeled. Plug the connector into either the COM1 or COM2 connectors. Be sure that pin 1 on the motherboard corresponds to pin 1 on the cable (colored line indicates pin 1).

The serial port is now ready for use.

STEP 20 Connect the parallel port to the motherboard

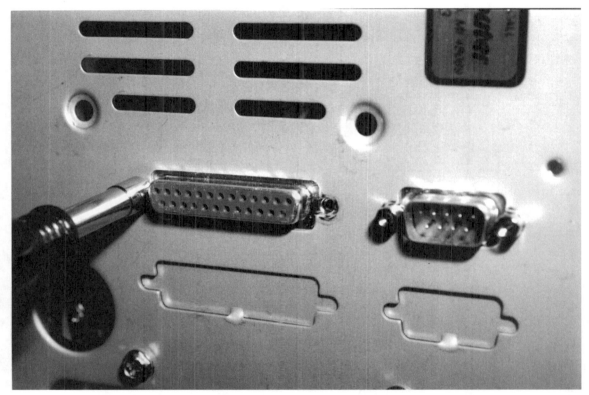

Figure 3.55   Secure the parallel port connector to the back of the case.

In addition to the two serial ports, the I/O capabilities of this motherboard (or separate I/O card) include a parallel port—sometimes called a printer port.

The parallel port is a 25-pin female connector that usually mounts onto the back panel of the case. Remove one of the knockouts for this connector size.

Mount the connector to the back panel of the case as in Figure 3.55. A flat ribbon runs between this connector and attaches to the motherboard with a 25-pin plastic connector. The motherboard connectors are usually clearly labeled with the word PARALLEL or PRINTER or LPT. Be sure that pin 1 on the motherboard corresponds to pin 1 on the cable (a colored line indicates pin 1).

The parallel port is now ready for use.

STEP 21
Connect the monitor to the video display card

We installed the video display card in our computer system in Step 16.

The 15-pin connector for the monitor is now at the back panel of the case. Plug the monitor cable into the video display card connector.

Finally, plug the monitor power cord into a grounded electrical outlet.

Figure 3.56 Connecting the monitor to the video display card.

STEP 22 · Connect the keyboard

The keyboard connector is attached directly to the motherboard. When you mount the motherboard in the case, the connector is aligned with a cutout in the case.

Plug the keyboard into the connector, as in the following figure:

Figure 3.57 Plug the keyboard cable into the keyboard connector on the back of the case.

Check and Double Check the Connections. Clean up.

We're almost ready to turn on the computer. But first, we're asking you to carefully inspect and review your work.

Go back and review Step 5 through Step 22.

This may seem like an unnecessary thing to do, but by rereading and inspecting your work, you will help ensure that you've done things correctly. Things that you want to especially look for:

❖ Make sure that the bottom side of the motherboard is not touching any metal parts.

❖ Look for loose wires that may be touching the motherboard. A short circuit can damage the system.

❖ Move unused power supply connectors away from other components. You can rubber band these to hold them out of the way.

STEP 24 — Turn on the Power

You're now ready to try out the new computer.

We assume the hard drive is new, has not been formatted and does not contain an operating system.

Remove any diskettes from the floppy drive.

Turn on the power to the monitor.

Next, turn on the power to the computer.

When we turned our computer on, first the video display card BIOS displays this message:

```
© 1995 Number Nine Visual Technology Corp
All rights reserved
#9-868 BIOS version 2.04.03
```

Then the BIOS on the motherboard displays these messages:

```
Award Modular BIOS V4.50PG. An Energy Star Ally
Copyright © 1994-95, Award Software, Inc.

03/13/1996 For i430HX PCIset

PENTIUM-S CPU at 166MHz
Memory Test: 16384K OK

Award Plug and Play BIOS Extension v1.0A
Copyright © 1995, Award Software, Inc.
   Detecting HDD Primary Master  WDC AC2120
```

Since this hard drive is brand new and is not yet formatted, the following message was displayed on the screen telling us that the BIOS is not able to load the operating system from the hard drive.

```
DISK BOOT FAILURE, INSERT SYSTEM DISK AND PRESS ENTER
```

Even though we haven't progressed very far, we have verified that the computer system is running. Make sure that the CPU cooling fan is operating correctly. If not, turn off the power and recheck the connections to the power supply.

Here are the startup screens for a second computer that we built. In this computer system, we used a Trident video display card. When we turned the power on, the video display card BIOS did not display any messages on the screen. We went directly to the messages from the motherboard BIOS:

```
Award Modular BIOS V4.50PG. An Energy Star Ally
Copyright © 1994-95, Award Software, Inc.


P5I437/250A BIOS V1.0 96-4-33


PENTIUM-S CPU at 166MHz
Memory Test: 16384K OK


Award Plug and Play BIOS Extension v1.0A
Copyright © 1995, Award Software, Inc.
   Detecting HDD Primary Master  WDC AC2120
```

Again, the hard drive does not contain a bootable operating system, so we see the following message:

```
DISK BOOT FAILURE, INSERT SYSTEM DISK AND PRESS ENTER
```

Even though we get these error messages, we have verified the computer is working properly. Success! Both of these computer systems are working. We can now move on. If you're still having trouble see the next page.

Before we move on to the final step on installing the operating system to the hard drive, you can now complete the assembly by closing the case. Carefully slide the cover onto the case and secure it with the hex screws — reversing the process of Step 3.

Now let's move to the final step of installing the operating system on the hard drive.

If You Have Trouble

Screen is blank when the system is turned on:

Things to check

- ❖ Power supply is not plugged into an electrical outlet.
- ❖ Monitor is not plugged into electrical outlet.
- ❖ Monitor is not turned on.
- ❖ Monitor is not connected to the video display card.
- ❖ Video display card is not properly seated in the motherboard slot.
- ❖ SIMMs are not properly seated in their sockets.
- ❖ SIMMs are not installed in pairs.
- ❖ Motherboard is not connected to power supply (P8 and P9 connectors).
- ❖ Floppy cable is not properly connected to the floppy drive.
- ❖ Floppy cable is not properly connected to the motherboard (or I/O card).
- ❖ Hard drive cable is not properly connected to the hard drive.
- ❖ Hard drive cable is not properly connected to the motherboard (or I/O card).
- ❖ Motherboard not grounded to the case. Make sure that the motherboard is firmly secured to the case using brass standoffs.

Screen displays BIOS startup message but then "hangs" before DOS is loaded

Things to check

- ❖ Hard drive is not plugged into IDE port.
- ❖ Power cable is not plugged into the hard drive.
- ❖ Power cable is not plugged into the floppy drive.
- ❖ Floppy drive is not plugged into the floppy controller cable.
- ❖ Floppy controller cable is plugged in backwards.
- ❖ Floppy drive is plugged into "B" connector instead of "A".
- ❖ Hard drive controller cable is plugged in backwards.
- ❖ Boot sequence for the hard drive should be A,C so it will load DOS from floppy drive This is specified by using BIOS setup. For our computer, to enter BIOS setup, press Del as the system is starting.

4

Putting Together A Pentium III Computer

4 Putting Together A Pentium III Computer

Now that you've selected and bought all of your components, you're ready to assemble your computer system. We've laid out a step by step approach that we've successfully used to build and rebuild many different computers. No matter how excited or impatient you are about building your new computer, please follow all of the steps in the order in which we've presented them. We don't want you to make a mistake that ends up "frying" one of the components.

WARNING

Electrical energy is dangerous. You should know that a computer is an electrical appliance. As such, you must take precautions against electrical shock. Always unplug the computer's power supply from the power outlet before you attempt to add, move or remove a component.

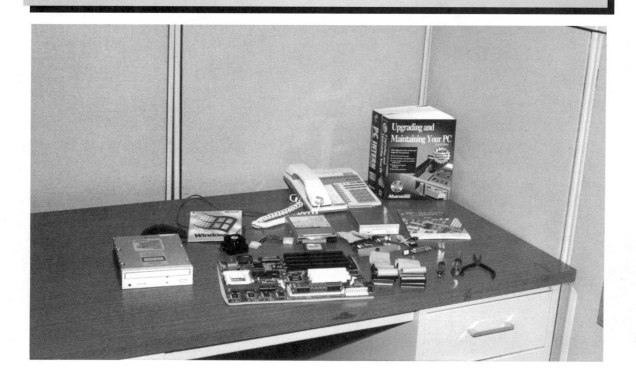

Prepare a work area

It's easier said than done, but make the effort to clear a flat, work area about six feet by four feet in size so that you can assemble your PC without falling all over yourself.

An oversized card table or an unused workbench or desk works well. The work surface should be clean. If the work surface cannot be washed, spread clean, white paper over the area. We don't recommend using newspaper because it's hard to find small parts when they drop on news articles and pictures.

The work area should be well lighted; it's usually dark when you're working inside a computer case and the extra light will make assembling your PC much easier. Stay away from drafty areas since small parts are likely to be blown away and lost.

Figure 4.2 A clear well-lighted work area speeds the assembly.

Gather your tools

Contrary to what you might think, you don't need very many tools to assemble a computer. Most of you will have the necessary tools already. Here's what you'll need:

❖ Phillips Screwdriver #1 head

❖ Screwdriver 1/8" blade

❖ Nutdriver 3/8"

❖ Long-nose pliers

❖ Several small paper cups (the small, bathroom size Dixie cups are great) for holding small screws and parts

❖ Large mouse pad or small hand towel on which to place the motherboard

❖ A pen and a pad of paper to take notes

❖ Hammer, to be used only when you can't get the computer to work—<u>JUST KIDDING</u>!

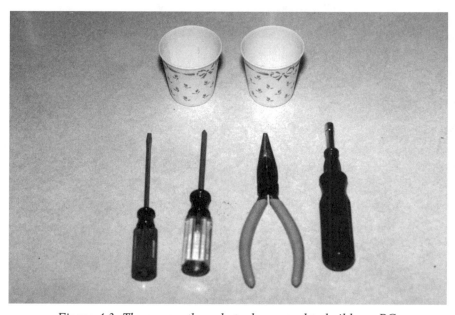

Figure 4.3 These were the only tools we used to build our PC.

If the only Phillips head screwdriver you own is too big or too small, then STOP. Go to a hardware store and buy one that's the correct size. You risk damaging the components or stripping the screw heads by using the wrong tool. A new tool costs only a few dollars. Compare this small expense to the amount of money that you've invested in your new computer.

<table>
<tr><td>**STEP 3**</td><td>**Prepare the case**</td></tr>
</table>

Start preparing the case by laying out the parts as needed. Let's start with our ATX case. First, remove it from the box. Take off the foam, the plastic bag and turn the case right side up. (Don't worry about the stuff moving around inside.)

Next, take a close look at the case. Notice the front has three 5.25-inch bays and two 3.5-inch bays. The back of the case has some vent holes, seven expansion slots, several screws holding the sides on and an ATX opening cover plate with some knockouts removed (see Figure 4.4). The back also has a power supply with fan and an emergency off switch and several knockouts still in place in the main part of the case.

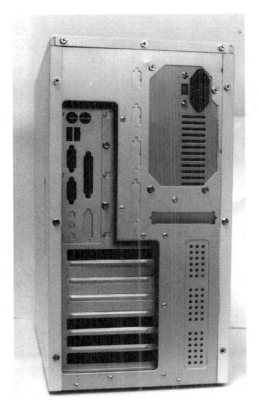

Figure 4.4 The back of the case has vent holes, expansion slots, screws holding the sides on and an ATX opening cover plate with some knockouts removed.

After you have identified all the parts, remove all the screws holding the sides on. Next, pull back gently on the sides. Start with one side and then pull on the other side (see Figure 4.5).

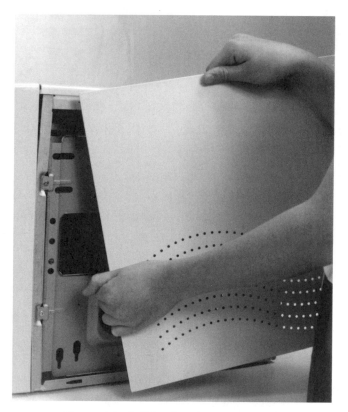

Figure 4.5 Pull back gently on the sides.

Remove anything from the inside that isn't tied down and put it together in a safe place. You should have removed a power cord, plastic standoffs, screws, brass standoffs, paper washers, and four self-adhesive rubber feet for the outside bottom of the case.

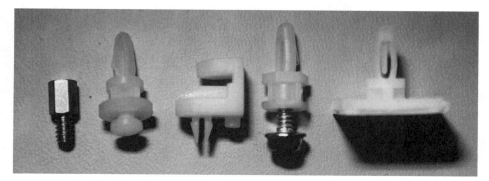

*Figure 4.6 Standoffs– from left to right Brass, Standard, Edge,
Screw down, and Adhesive backed.
(Courtesy of Skyline Computers, Brookfield, IL)*

Keep everything you removed for later. The front cooling fan and the speaker remain.

Pull off the front of the case (see Figure 4.7). This might be the FIRST step to disassembling your case! Sometimes the front is held on with screws on the inside. Be sure to remove them.

Figure 4.7 Removing the front of the case.

Next, we remove the top panel. Remove all the metal plates in the bays in front of the case. Do this by wiggling them back and forth until they fall out (but don't force them). The points on the plates where they were attached will be sharp. However, if you force them, the sharp points stay with the case instead.

Next, hold up the front panel and choose a location for the CD-ROM and the floppy drive. Pop out the covers from the back. It doesn't matter which ones you choose; they can be moved later if necessary. Throw away the metal plates and the two covers since they're no longer needed.

Unscrew the large plate on the side and tip it out. This is the mounting plate for the motherboard. Finally, remove the two screws holding in the ATX plate.

Remove the plate and put it in a safe place. We have now stripped our case.

Electrostatic energy (we used to call it static electricity) is capable of damaging computer circuits in some of the components. To prevent damaging them, you'll need to discharge yourself of this deadly "disease" before handling the components.

A simple way to do this is to ground yourself. When your power supply is plugged into a three-prong wall outlet, the computer case is also grounded. To discharge yourself of the electrostatic energy, touch the metal computer case.

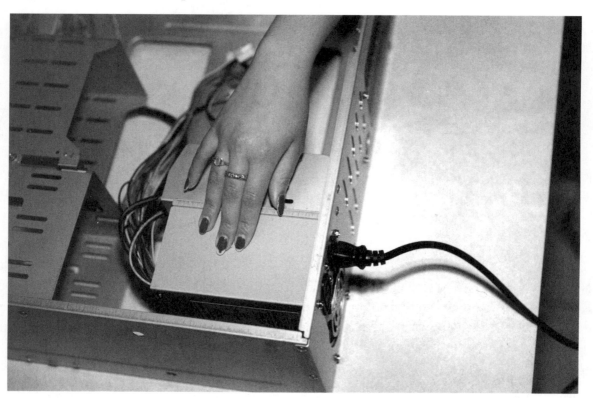

Figure 4.9 You can discharge yourself of electrostatic energy by grounding yourself to the case.

Another way to discharge yourself of electrostatic energy is to wear a wrist strap. This device is like a watch with a leash. The leash is connected to a ground and the other end wraps around your wrist. You're always grounded by wearing the wrist strap.

The next step is to *configure* or set up the motherboard. You'll now have to <u>carefully read the user's manual</u> for your motherboard. You'll have to find the instructions for setting any DIP switches and/or jumpers for the computer that you are about to build. Before you get started, we'll cover a few basics that will be helpful.

DIP switches are usually found in sets of from two to eight miniature light switches on a small plastic base which is soldered to the top of the motherboard. The individual switches are numbered and the label on the plastic base indicates whether a given switch is on or off. To turn a switch on, use a ball-point pen to move the switch in the **ON** direction. To turn a switch off, move the switch **opposite the ON** direction. The image on the right shows how a row of DIP switches appears on a motherboard.

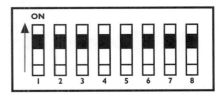

Figure 4.10 A DIP switch that might be found on a motherboard.

A jumper is another kind of switch. You'll notice that there are several metal pins sticking up from the surface of the motherboard. The pins are labeled JP1 or J10, for example. A jumper cap is a small metal connector surrounded by insulated plastic (most jumper caps are black in color). When you put the jumper cap on two of the pins, you *close* or *turn on* the switch. If you don't put a jumper cap on the pins, then the switch is *open* or *turned off*. In some cases the pins on the motherboard are paired and labeled 1 and 2; in other cases, there may be three pins labeled 1, 2 and 3. You may be asked to select one option by jumpering pins 1 and 2 or other option by jumpering pins 2 and 3.

Side View   **Top View**

Jumper Cap

Jumper

1 2 3

P I N

Figure 4.11 This is a typical jumper on a motherboard.

The setting in Figure 4.11 is made by jumpering pins 2 and 3.

In this book we also refer to a *connector*. In one instance, a connector may refer to a set of pins on the motherboard (usually from 2 to 40 pins). A connector may also refer to the black plastic plug at the end of a set of wires or cable which is attached to the pins.

Consult the owner's manual that came with your motherboard. The following diagram (Figure 4.12) from our owners manual shows where all the components are on the motherboard.

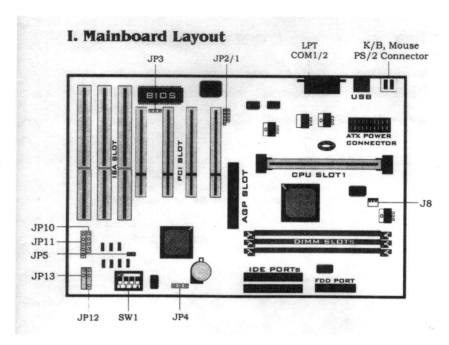

Figure 4.12 This diagram (Figure 4.12) from our owners manual shows the location of the components on the motherboard.

After you have identified all the components of the motherboard, take your removed ATX plate and line it up with the openings on the board. Remove any of the knockouts necessary to expose the component. Check the fit like the following:

Now, reinstall the ATX plate and throw away the knockouts. The back of your case should look like that in Figure 4.14.

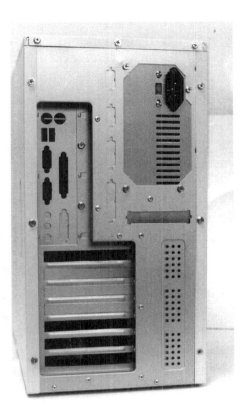

Figure 4.14. This is how the back of your case should appear.

Now, turn your attention back to the motherboard. We need to set the CPU clock. Our chip is 300 MHz, so we consult the table in our manual. We need the 66 X 4.5 setting, so we set switches 2 and 4 to the "on" position.

Warning: Don't set the speed too high. It will VOID the warranty on your CPU. The CPU may overheat, and most vendors will not accept CPUs for return that have been overheated. For this reason, always use a quality cooling fan.

III. CPU Setting

1. CPU Ratio Setting (SW1)

	1	2	3	4
2	ON	ON	ON	ON
2				
2.5	ON	ON		ON
3	ON		ON	ON
3.5	ON			ON
4		ON	ON	ON
4.5		ON		ON
5			ON	ON

Null: OFF

2. CPU External Clock

Refer to Chipset Features Setup and setup in 66MHz.

Intel	Speed & Ratio
233	66 x 3.5
266	66 x 4
300	66 x 4.5
333	66 x 5

STEP 6 — Assemble the CPU, fan and heat sink

Next, let's prepare the Pentium II chip. We need to install the heat sink/fan unit, and we need to attach the bracket to the motherboard. Here's the front and the back of the chip. Notice several holes in the back of the chip, but pay special attention to the four rectangular holes marked in this picture. These are used for attaching the two CPU fan clips (they run top to bottom).

Figure 4.16 This is the Pentium II (left) and the two slots for the CPU fan clips (right).

First, place the CPU fan against the metal side of the CPU. The notches will guide you, but be sure the heat sink sits evenly spaced top to bottom to avoid covering the holes for the clips. Attach the clips and secure the fan/heat sink to the CPU.

Figure 4.17 Attach the clips and secure the fan/heat sink to the CPU.

Next, we need to determine which direction the bracket needs to face upon installation on the motherboard.

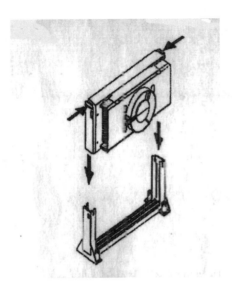

Figure 4.18 Slide the CPU into the CPU bracket.
Make certain the notch on each side lines up with the clip.

Slide the CPU into the CPU bracket making sure the notch on each side lines up with the clip.
If it doesn't, turn the bracket around.

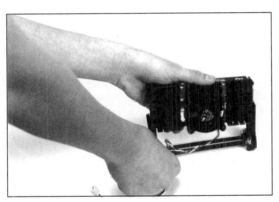

Install the CPU and bracket on the motherboard

Look at the motherboard and be certain the fan faces the large open space.

*Figure 4.20 Make certain the studs show through the holes
(indicated inside the white rectaangle in this illustration).*

Follow the diagram in the manual and position the CPU bracket mounts on the underside of the motherboard.

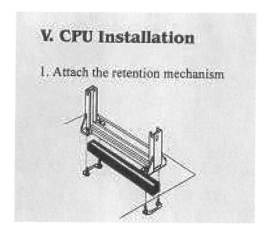

Turn over the motherboard but be careful not to lose the mounts. Place the motherboard on your work surface. Place the CPU/Bracket/Fan assembly on the motherboard, aligning the nuts in the bracket with the mount studs, and facing the CPU in the correct direction.

Attach the cooling fan connector to the motherboard (see following figure).

Figure 4.24 Attaching the cooling fan.

Next, push in the CPU locking clips (one on each side).

Figure 4.25 Pushing in the CPU locking clips.

Then pull out the CPU while holding down the bracket. The bracket is now facing the right direction. Using a Phillips head screwdriver, gently tighten each of the four brass nuts.

Figure 4.26 Make certain to tighten each of the four brass nuts.

Finally, install the CPU again and lock it in place.

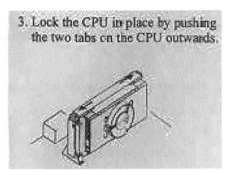

3. Lock the CPU in place by pushing the two tabs on the CPU outwards.

Congratulations! You just installed a Pentium II!

We'll install the memory in this step. Figure 4.28 shows the DIMM. Notice the two notches on the bottom. These notches will prevent you from installing it the wrong way in the slot.

Figure 4.28   Example of DIMM (Dual Inline Memory Module).

The DIMM slots have tabs that push down. These only help you remove the DIMM, it doesn't matter what position they are in when you push in the DIMM, they'll pop in and up towards the module.

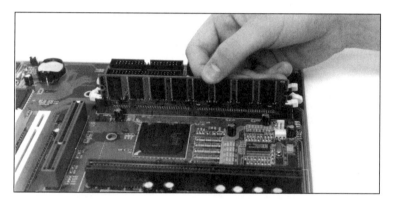

Be certain to install the DIMM in Bank 0. It will be clearly marked on the motherboard or in the manual. Simply push it in when you're ready. To remove a DIMM, simply push down and out on the tabs. The DIMM will pop out into your hands.

Congratulations—you're done with the memory. Figure 4.30 shows the motherboard with the CPU and the DIMM installed.

Figure 4.30   The motherboard with the CPU and DIMM installed.

STEP 9

Mount the motherboard to the plate

Lay the board on the plate lining up the motherboard holes with the plate below it.

Install a brass standoff in any threaded plate hole that has a corresponding motherboard hole with a metal ring.

Slot 1 motherboards are designed to support a variety of fan types. Your fan may use the optional secondary support bracket if it is large. There are two holes in the motherboard for this. Don't put standoffs or screws in them or it will be difficult to install a larger fan later. They are located adjacent to the CPU slot, on the fan side:

Some plates have notches for plastic standoffs:

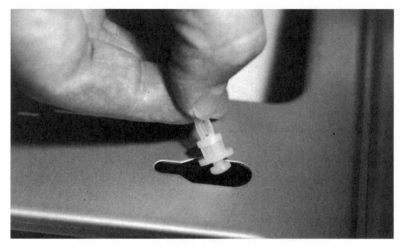

Figure 4.33   Slide the standard plastic standoff into the oblong cutout in the chassis.

Note: For any other holes in the motherboard that don't have a corresponding threaded hole in the plate, you may cut the bottom off of a standoff, install a self-adhesive standoff (available separately), or drill and tap a hole, then install a brass standoff and screw. However, keep in mind that computers sit still and you may not need to support the motherboard at every point. As long as the motherboard is supported evenly, you don't have to worry about one or two holes that are not supported.

If You Have Trouble

Sometimes the holes in the motherboard just will not line up with the cutouts and screw holes on the chassis.

If this happens, you can purchase either screw down standoffs or adhesive backed standoffs. Either of these standoffs can be placed anywhere on the chassis. For screw down standoffs, you'll have to drill a hole in the desired position on the chassis. For the adhesive backed standoffs, you can remove the protective backing and press the standoff in the desired position.

Note: At least one of your mounts should be a metal standoff and a screw in a hole that has the metal ring! This provides a complete path from the motherboard to the power supply, and prevents the buildup of static electricity on the motherboard.

Now, insert one screw in each hole to attach the motherboard to the plate.

Gently tighten the screws, but again, start all before finishing any.

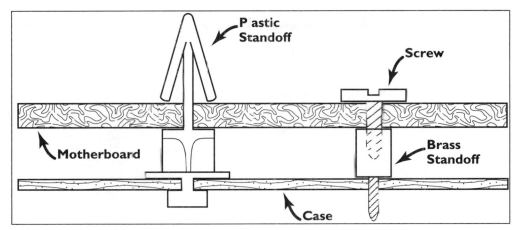

Figure 4.34 This side view shows you how the plastic and brass standoffs are used to mount the motherboard to the chassis.

STEP 10 Install the floppy drive

Lay the motherboard down near the case like in Figure 4.35. The front panel of your case has several removable plastic or metal plates covering the drive bays. The narrow plates cover the bays for 3.5-inch drives while the wider plates cover the bays for 5.25-inch drives.

These plates can be removed from the front panel by gently popping them out from the front panel. Remove one of the plates for your 3.5-inch floppy drive (see Figure 4.36).

Next slide the floppy drive into one of the 3.5-inch bays so that the front of the drive is flush with the front (see Figure 4.37). Then secure the drive to the case with at least four screws. You may have to flip the case on its other side to secure both sides of the drive to the mounting brackets.

Figure 4.35 The motherboard is attached to the removable sidewall of the case..

Figure 4.37 Slide the floppy drive into the case from the front.

Figure 4.36 Remove the face plate from the front cover of the case.

A 34-wire ribbon cable is used to connect the floppy drive to the motherboard (or I/O card). In Figure 4.37, you can see that one end of the cable connects to the floppy controller on either the motherboard or a separate I/O board.

The other end has two connectors for the floppy drive. One of these is for a floppy drive that has an edge connector and the other is for a floppy drive that has a 34-pin connector. See Figure 4.38.

In the middle are two connectors for the B drive. Again, one is for an edge connector and the other for a 34-pin connector.

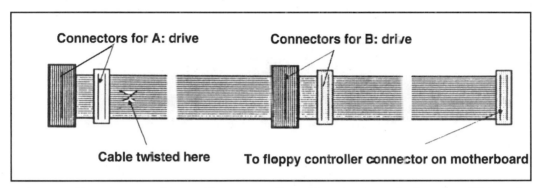

Figure 4.38 A 34-wire ribbon cable connects floppy drive to the motherboard or I/O board.

Most likely, your floppy drive will have a 34-pin connector since the edge connectors are ancient. In any case, plug either the 34-pin connector or the edge connector into the back of the floppy drive. The edge connector on the ribbon is "keyed" so it will fit onto the floppy drive in only one direction. Then plug one of the power supply connectors into the back of the floppy drive as in Figure 4.40.

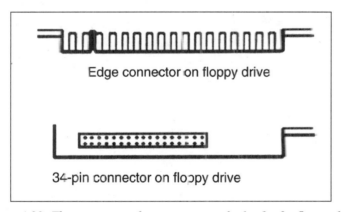

Figure 4.39 The two types of connectors on the back of a floppy drive.

Along the length of the cable is a color line which indicates pin 1 on the connector. Plug the 34-pin connector into the floppy controller port on the motherboard (or separate I/O board) making sure that pin 1 of the connector matches pin 1 on the board. See Figure 4.41.

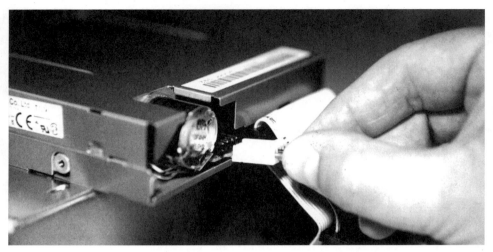

Figure 4.40 Plug the power supply cable and the 34-pin connector (A-drive) into the floppy drive.

Figure 4.41 Plug the 34-pin ribbon cable from the floppy drive to the motherboard (or separate I/O card).

STEP 11 — Install the hard drive

Since the hard drive will be totally enclosed within the case, you won't have to remove a plastic or metal plate from the case's front panel to install your hard drive. Slide the hard drive into one of the bays so that the connectors on the drive are accessible. Secure the hard drive to the case with four screws.

A 40-wire ribbon cable is used to connect the hard drive to the motherboard (or I/O card). The ribbon cable has three 40-pin connectors—one at each end and a third about one-third of the way towards one end (see Figure 4.42).

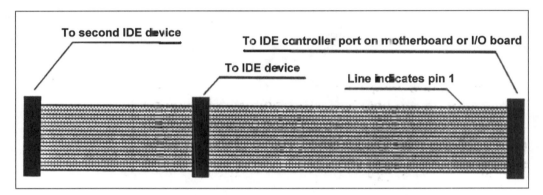

To second IDE device

To IDE controller port on motherboard or I/O board

To IDE device

Line indicates pin 1

Figure 4.42 A 40-wire ribbon cable connects IDE devices to the motherboard or I/O board.

Plug the other end of the cable into connector on the hard drive, again making sure that pin 1 on the cable matches pin 1 of the hard drive. Plug one of the power supply connectors into the hard drive (see Figure 4.43 on the following page).

A color line (usually red) along the length of the cable ribbon indicates pin 1, similar to the 34-pin floppy cable. Plug one end of the 40-pin connectors into the primary IDE controller connector on the motherboard (or separate I/O board) making sure that pin 1 of the connector matches pin 1 on the board (see Figure 4.44 on the following page).

Figure 4.43 Plug the 40-pin connector and the power supply connector into the back of the hard drive.

Figure 4.44 Plug the 40-pin connector into the motherboard (or separate I/O card).

STEP 12 Install the CD-ROM drive

Remove one of the plastic or metal plates from the front panel that covers a 5.25-inch bay. Regardless of the make of an IDE CD-ROM drive, they are configured similarly. To be absolutely sure, you'll want to refer to the CD-ROM drive installation manual. Our explanation is a general one, but it should be similar to that from your installation manual.

An IDE device—hard drive or CD-ROM drive—is set as a master device or a slave device by setting a jumper on the rear of the drive. If the IDE controller port already has one device attached (our computer already has the hard drive connected), then that device (the hard drive) is the master and the second device (the CD-ROM) is the slave. Therefore, set the jumper on the CD-ROM drive which makes it a slave. This is usually the default setting from the factory.

After you set the jumper, slide the CD-ROM drive into the bay so that the front of the CD-ROM drive is flush with the front. Secure the CD-ROM drive to the case with four screws. Locate the middle 40-pin connector on the ribbon cable and plug it into the back of the CD-ROM drive as you align pin 1 of the connector to pin 1 of the CD-ROM drive. Plug a 4-wire power cable into the power connector on the CD-ROM drive. See Figure 4.45.

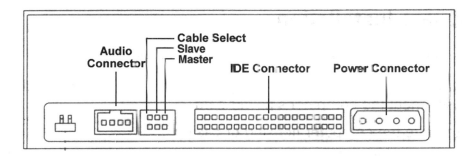

Figure 4.45 The back of a typical IDE CD-ROM drive.

Alternative:

You can also connect the CD-ROM to the secondary IDE controller port. If no other devices are connected to the secondary IDE controller, then you would set the jumper on the CD-ROM drive which makes it a master. Some manufacturers recommend that you use this setup so the performance of a hard drive sharing the same cable is not adversely affected by the slower CD-ROM transfer rate.

If you choose this method, you must use a second 40-pin ribbon cable and plug one connector into the secondary IDE port and the other end into the CD-ROM drive.

In order to hear audio through your sound card, you'll have to connect the CD-ROM drive to the sound card with an audio cable. One end of the cable attaches to the rear of the CD-ROM drive and the other plugs into the sound card.

STEP 13
Connect the other wires to the motherboard

Here is each case connector, each clearly labeled:

Next, attach the connectors to the motherboard. Attach each connector according to the labels on the motherboard, using the chart and diagram in the manual as a guide.

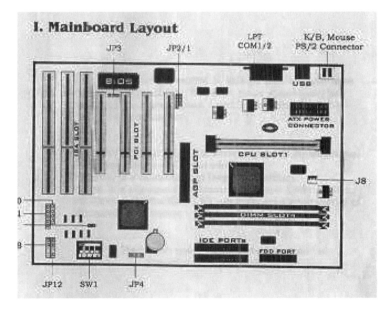

II. Jumper & Setting

JP1 : Consumer IR
JP2 : IR
JP3 : 1-2 5V Flush ROM
      2-3 12V Flush ROM
JP4 : 1-2 Default
      2-3 Clear CMOS
JP5 : ATX ON/OFF SW
J8 : CPU Fan Connector
JP10: 1-2 HDD LED
JP11: 1-3 Power LED
      4-5 Keylock
JP12: Speaker
JP13: Reset SW

Not all connectors will be used; for example, our case has a "Turbo" connector for a 486 motherboard. We don't need it. Also, we aren't using IR(infrared) or a keylock.

STEP 14
Install the motherboard plate and connect the power supply

Locate the power connector on the motherboard:

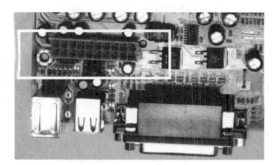

It corresponds to the large ATX power connector (multi-colored, has about 20 wires) coming from the power supply:

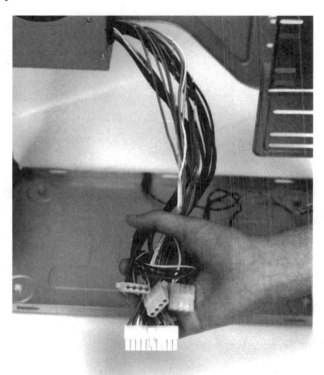

For alignment, the motherboard and the power supply end have a notch and a clip, respectively. For our case, we will install the motherboard power connector as we install the motherboard. Now, we reinstall the plate with the motherboard, tilting it in the opposite way it came out.

We pause to connect the power supply as we tip the motherboard into place:

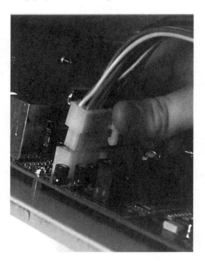

Now, attach the screws and secure the plate to the case.

Pause: Tips For Installing Add-on Cards

Before we continue, we want to take a short break to explain how to install add-on cards in the expansion slots on the motherboard. In some computer cases, the expansion slot covers are stamped into the case's back panel. To remove a slot cover, carefully bend it back and forth until the bottom "tears" away from the panel. As you do this, be careful not to damage any of the tiny components on the motherboard. Figure 4.53 below shows how you remove one of the expansion slot covers.

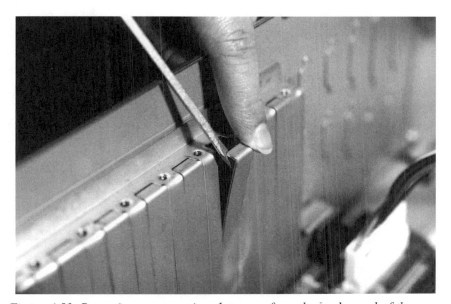

Figure 4.53 Removing an expansion slot cover from the back panel of the case.

In other computer cases, the expansion slot covers are screwed into the back panel. To remove a slot cover, unscrew the screw holding the cover in place.

Tips
Here are tips to follow when installing any card into an expansion slot:
❖ Carefully insert the edge of the card into the slot.   ❖ Rock the board back and forth slightly from front to back until it seats securely in the slot and the metal fingers are making positive contact.   ❖ Check that no part of the card is pressing on any of the delicate motherboard components underneath.   ❖ Verify that the metal plate on the card aligns perfectly with the back of the case.   ❖ Screw the metal plate into the case to complete the physical installation.

Now we're ready to connect the peripherals. This motherboard has built-in onboard I/O. You may have bought a separate I/O card. If so, you can insert it into one of the ISA slots on the motherboard and secure it with a screw to the back of the case. In subsequent steps, when we refer to "connectors on the motherboard," you should substitute "connectors on the I/O board."

If you've removed the cage, you can now reinstall it since the motherboard is securely seated in the case.

Here are the cables that attach the peripherals to the motherboard:

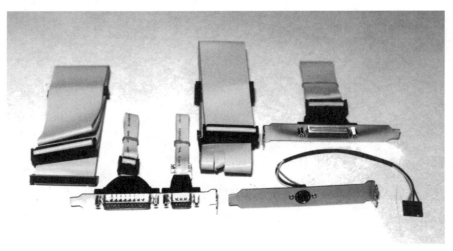

Figure 4.54 Here's all the connecting cables that you'll use to attach peripherals to the motherboard.

STEP 15 | Install the video display card

Your motherboard may have one brown AGP slot, four or five white PCI slots, and from two to four black ISA slots. Insert your video card into the corresponding slot (AGP or PCI). Use a screw to secure the card to the back of the case:

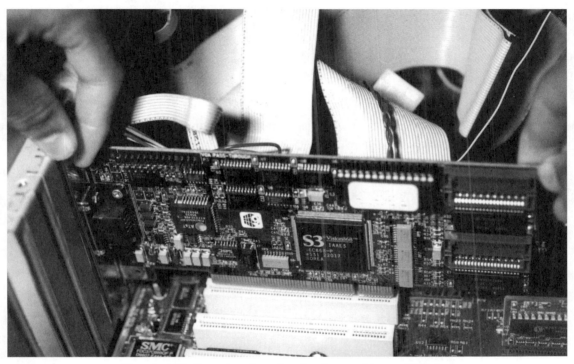

Figure 4.55 Inserting the video display card into a PCI slot.

STEP 16 Install the sound card

Because we've selected a Plug 'n' Play sound card, there aren't any jumpers or switches that we have to set on this card.

If you are installing a conventional sound card (not Plug 'n Play), then you may have to set jumpers or switches so that the operation of the sound card does not interfere with the operation of any other devices connected to the computer. Since there are so many different sound cards, we can't tell you how to configure any particular sound card, but the default settings are often a good place to start. Creative Labs Sound Blaster and compatible cards usually have a default of I/O port address 220, IRQ 5, DMA 1 which usually work well.

Insert the sound card into one of the ISA slots. Secure the card to back of the case with a screw. Plug the speakers into the sound card.

Refer to the sound card installation manual to locate the CD audio connector. Plug the audio cable from the CD-ROM into the CD audio connector on the sound card.

STEP 17 — Front fan

Connect the front panel case fan power connector. It connects to any drive power connector and has an additional connector for a drive.

STEP
18
Connect the monitor to the video display card

We installed the video display card in our computer system in Step 16.

The 15-pin connector for the monitor is now at the back panel of the case. Plug the monitor cable into the video display card connector.

Finally, plug the monitor power cord into a grounded electrical outlet.

Figure 4.56 Connecting the monitor.

The keyboard connector is attached directly to the motherboard. When you mount the
motherboard in the case, the connector is aligned with a cutout in the case.

STEP 19 Connect the keyboard

The keyboard connector is attached directly to the motherboard. When you mount the
motherboard in the case, the connector is aligned with a cutout in the case.

Plug the keyboard into the connector as in Figure 4.57:

Figure 4.57 Plug the keyboard cable into the keyboard connector on the back of the case.

The PS/2 style connector for the mouse is mounted onto a metal expansion slot cover. A narrow
ribbon cable (or wire harness) runs between this connector and the motherboard.

Plug the six-pin connector into the appropriate connector on the motherboard (for our
motherboard it's J10), making sure that pin 1 on the motherboard corresponds to pin 1 on the
connector (a colored line indicates pin 1). Next mount the expansion slot cover with the mouse
port onto the back panel of the case (see Figure 4.53).

Finally, plug the mouse into the mouse port (see Figure 4.59).

Figure 4.58 Securing the mouse port to the case.

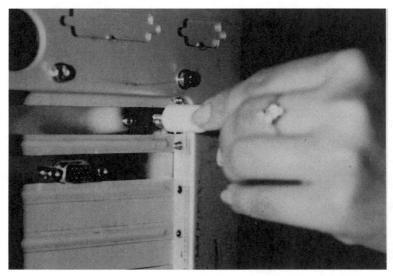

Figure 4.59 Plug the mouse in the PS/2 mouse port.

STEP 20 — Check and double check the connections and then clean up

We're almost ready to turn on the computer. But first, we're asking you to carefully inspect and review your work.

Go back and review Step 5 through Step 19.

This may seem like an unnecessary thing to do, but by rereading and inspecting your work, you will help ensure that you've done things correctly. Things that you want to especially look for:

❖ Make sure that the bottom side of the motherboard is not touching any metal parts.

❖ Look for loose wires that may be touching the motherboard. A short circuit can damage the system.

❖ Move unused power supply connectors away from other components. You can rubber band these to hold them out of the way.

TIP: Once you are satisfied that the computer is in good working order, then reinstall the cover on the case! Otherwise, you may have to remove it again right away.

Turn on the power

You're now ready to try out the new computer. Place the emergency shut-off switch on the back of the power supply to the on position. You'll only need this switch if the PC's power needs to be cut in a hurry. (If the operating system is not responding, use the reset button on the front). To switch on the computer, press the ⟨Spacebar⟩ (if your motherboard supports this feature and it is enabled in the BIOS) or the ATX power button on the front of the case. Don't use the ATX power button to turn off the computer. Windows 95 and 98 will turn off the computer automatically after you choose **Shut Down** on the **Start** menu (if enabled in the BIOS and in the OS).

We assume the hard drive is new, has not been formatted and does not contain an operating system. Remove any diskettes from the floppy drive.

Switch on the power to the monitor. Next, switch on the power to the computer.

When we turned our computer on, first the video display card BIOS displays this message:

© 1995 Number Nine Visual Technology Corp
All rights reserved
#9-868 BIOS version 2.04.03

Then the BIOS on the motherboard displays these messages:

Award Modular BIOS V4.50PG. An Energy Star Ally
Copyright © 1994-95, Award Software, Inc.

03/13/1996 For i430HX PCIset

PENTIUM-S II at 233 MHz
Memory Test: 16384K OK

Award Plug and Play BIOS Extension v1.0A
Copyright © 1995, Award Software, Inc.
  Detecting HDD Primary Master WDC AC2120

Since this hard drive is brand new and is not yet formatted, the following message was displayed on the screen telling us that the BIOS is not able to load the operating system from the hard drive.

DISK BOCT FAILURE, INSERT SYSTEM DISK AND PRESS ENTER

Although we haven't progressed very far, we have verified that the computer system is running. Make sure that the CPU cooling fan is operating correctly. If not, turn off the power and recheck the connections to the power supply.

Although we get these error messages, we have verified the computer is working properly. Success! Our computer system is working. We can now move on. If you're still having trouble see the next page.

Before we move on to the final step on installing the operating system to the hard drive, you can now complete the assembly by closing the case. Carefully slide the cover onto the case and secure it with the hex screws — reversing the process of Step 3.

Now let's move to the final step of installing the operating system on the hard drive.

If You Have Trouble

Screen is blank when the system is turned on:

Things to check

- ❖ Power supply is not plugged into an electrical outlet.
- ❖ Monitor is not plugged into electrical outlet.
- ❖ Monitor is not turned on.
- ❖ Monitor is not connected to the video display card.
- ❖ Video display card is not properly seated in the motherboard slot.
- ❖ SIMMs are not properly seated in their sockets.
- ❖ SIMMs are not installed in pairs.
- ❖ Motherboard is not connected to power supply (P8 and P9 connectors).
- ❖ Floppy cable is not properly connected to the floppy drive.
- ❖ Floppy cable is not properly connected to the motherboard (or I/O card).
- ❖ Hard drive cable is not properly connected to the hard drive.
- ❖ Hard drive cable is not properly connected to the motherboard (or I/O card).
- ❖ Motherboard not grounded to the case. Make sure that the motherboard is firmly secured to the case using brass standoffs.

Screen displays BIOS startup message but then "hangs" before DOS is loaded

Things to check

- ❖ Hard drive is not plugged into IDE port.
- ❖ Power cable is not plugged into the hard drive.
- ❖ Power cable is not plugged into the floppy drive.
- ❖ Floppy drive is not plugged into the floppy controller cable.
- ❖ Floppy controller cable is plugged in backwards.
- ❖ Floppy drive is plugged into "B" connector instead of "A".
- ❖ Hard drive controller cable is plugged in backwards.
- ❖ Boot sequence for the hard drive should be A,C so it will load DOS from floppy drive This is specified by using BIOS setup. For our computer, to enter BIOS setup, press Del as the system is starting.

5

Installing The Operating System

5 Installing The Operating System

Now that the computer system is working, we must install the operating system. With all of the power in our new PC, we have the hardware to run Windows 95 or Windows 98.

The current version of Windows is Windows 98 (2nd edition). This new version of Windows includes the most current drivers and will support USB ports.

To install Windows, we'll take an approach that keeps installation problems to a minimum. We've used the following method to install and reinstall Windows on many computers. It isn't the most direct route to Windows, but it is very effective.

Our approach is to get both the CD-ROM drive and sound card to work under DOS. After we do this, then we are pretty much assured that they will also work under Windows. We'll use the following to install Windows:

1. Boot diskette containing DOS 6.x operating system. The diskette must be bootable and contain the following files:

   COMMAND.COM

   IO.SYS

   MSDOS.SYS

   FDISK.COM

   FORMAT.COM

   SYS.COM

   MSCDEX.EXE

2. Installation diskette for your CD-ROM drive

3. Installation diskette for your sound card

4. Windows CD-ROM.

Here's an outline of how we're going to install Windows onto your new computer:

1. Boot the computer using the bootable diskette from floppy drive A:

2. Partition the hard drive to make space for an operating system.

3. Format the hard drive and copy the MS-DOS operating system to it.

4. Copy the other files from the floppy diskette to the hard drive.

5. Install the software to access the CD-ROM drive.

6. Install Windows from the CD-ROM.

Let's get started.

Insert the bootable MS-DOS floppy diskette into drive A:

Turn on the computer

MS-DOS will load from the floppy and display the **A:>** prompt.

At the prompt type:

```
A:> fdisk (Enter)
```

The FDISK program will start and you'll see this screen:

```
                    MS-DOS Version 6
                    Fixed Disk Setup Program
                    ©Copyright Microsoft Corp. 1983-1993

                    FDISK Options

    Choose one of the following

      1  Create DOS Partition or Logical DOS Drive
      2  Set active partition
      3  Delete partition or Logical DOS Drive
      4  Display partition information

    Enter choice [1]

    Press Esc to exit FDISK
```

Since we want to create a new DOS partition on this hard drive, type 1 and press Enter.

Now this screen appears:

```
                    MS-DOS Version 6
                    Fixed Disk Setup Program
                    ©Copyright Microsoft Corp. 1983-1993

                    FDISK Options

    Choose one of the following

      1  Create Primary DOS partition
      2  Create Extended DOS partition
      3  Create Logical DOS Drive(s) in the Extended DOS partition


    Enter choice [1]

    Press Esc to exit FDISK
```

We need a Primary DOS Partition, so type 1 again and press Enter. You'll see the following screen:

```
                    MS-DOS Version 6
                  Fixed Disk Setup Program
               ©Copyright Microsoft Corp. 1983-1993

                       FDISK Options

      Choose one of the following

      1  Create Primary DOS partition

      Do you wish to use the maximum available size for a Primary DOS Partition
      and make the partition active (Y/N)?


      Enter choice [1]

   Press Esc to exit FDISK
```

We will use the entire hard drive for the new partition, so type Y and press Enter.

FDISK will allocate the entire hard drive space to the new partition and displays this final message:

```
      System will now restart
      Insert DOS system diskette in Drive A:
      Press any key when ready ...
```

Press any key and DOS will reload from your floppy diskette.

Before we use the hard drive, we first have to format the drive. Type the following, making sure that you include the switch /s that transfers the MS-DOS operating system from the floppy diskette to the hard drive:

```
A:> format c: /s  Enter
```

Note: The /s is important because it tells DOS to transfer system files to the hard drive.

The FORMAT program will start and display this warning message before it writes over any data which may have been previously written to the hard drive:

```
      WARNING: ALL DATA ON NON-REMOVABLE DISK
      DRIVE C: WILL BE LOST!
      Proceed with Format (Y/N)?
```

Assuming that this is a new hard drive, no data will be lost, so type Ⓨ and press [Enter].

The hard drive is then formatted and the minimal MS-DOS system is transferred to the hard drive. When FORMAT is almost done, you'll be asked to enter a label identifier for the newly formatted hard drive:

> Volume Label (11 character, ENTER for none)?

You can type an 11 character name, for example:

```
DRIVE_C [Enter]
```

Now that the hard drive is formatted, change to that drive:

```
A:>   c: [Enter]
```

Copy the other files from diskette to the hard drive by typing:

```
A:> copy a:*.* c: [Enter]
```

Next, remove the floppy diskette from drive A.

Press the reset switch on the case or turn the power off and then back on again to boot the computer from the hard drive. MS-DOS will load again, this time from the hard drive, and will display the **C:>** prompt.

```
C:>
```

Now we'll install the software to access the CD-ROM drive. The drivers and setup programs are supplied on a floppy diskette with your CD-ROM drive. You'll probably have to run a program from the diskette named SETUP (SETUPD) or INSTALL. The instruction manual for the CD-ROM will tell you the exact name.

Before running the INSTALL program for the Creative Labs 16 Plug 'n Play sound card, we had to install the Plug and Play Configuration Manager. This set of three floppy diskettes is needed for any Plug and Play devices - sound cards, modems, etc. This screen was displayed when we installed the PnP Configuration Manager:

> Plug and Play for MS-DOS® and Windows ™ Configuration Manager - R1.43
>
> Copyright 1993, 1994, 1995 Intel Corporation ALL RIGHTS RESERVED
>
> MS-DOS is a registered trademark and Windows is a trademark of Microsoft Corp.
>
> Found Plug and Play ISA card: Creative SB16 PnP
>
> The Plug and Play ISA card has been successfully configured

After Plug and Play installation, we can install the sound card software. The setup program is supplied on a floppy diskette for our sound card. You'll probably have to run a program from the diskette named SETUP or INSTALL. The instruction manual for the sound card will tell you the exact name.

Reboot the computer to try out the sound card.

With the CD-ROM and the sound card successfully installed, we can now install Windows.

Insert the Windows CD-ROM into the CD-ROM drive. Change to the CD-ROM drive by typing thee following:

D:⏎

Now start the Windows installation by typing:

D:> setup ⏎

The Windows installation will begin. Follow the directions on the screen to install a full version of Windows. When installation is complete, you will be asked to reboot your computer. Now you're on your own!

CONGRATULATIONS. You've graduated from computer building school and are ready to start using your brand new PC with Windows.

6

Getting More Information

6 Getting More Information

Books

Upgrading & Maintaining Your PC, 6th Edition written by Data Becker; published by Abacus, 1996, ISBN 1-55755-350-5, $44.95 w/ CD-ROM

Upgrading and Repairing PCs, 5th Edition written by Scott Mueller; published by Que, 1995, ISBN 0-7897-0321-1, $49.95 w/CD-ROM

Win 98 Rx written by Kober, Buechel and Baecker; published by Abacus, 1998, ISBN 1-55755-349-1, $34.95 w/CD-ROM

The Winn L. Rosch Hardware Bible, 3rd Edition written by Winn Rosch; published by SAMs Publishing, 1994, ISBN 1-56686-127-6, $35.00.

Upgrade & Maintain your PC written by James Karney; published by MID Press, ISBN 1-55828-294-7, 1994, $34.95 w/diskette

The Complete PC Upgrade & Maintenance Guide written by Mark Minasi; published by Sybex, 1993, $24.95.

Win 95 Rx written by Kober, Buechel and Baecker; published by Abacus, 1996, ISBN 1-55755-297-5, $34.95 w/CD-ROM

PC BIOS written by Data Becker; published by Abacus, 2000, ISBN 1-55755-342-4, $29.95 w/CD-ROM

PC Intern – Hardware Bible written by Michael Tischer; published by Abacus, 1998, ISBN 1-55755-351-3, $69.95 w/CD-ROM

PC Tuning; published by Abacus, 1998, ISBN 1-55755-341-6, $29.95 w/CD-ROM

Other References

Byte Magazine
One Phoenix Mill Lane
Peterborough, NH 03458
Phone: (603) 924-9281
Toll free: (800) 257-9402
Fax: (603) 924-2550
http://www.byte.com

Compu-Mart Magazine
899 Presidential
Suite 110
Richardson, TX 75081
Phone: (214) 238-1133
Toll free: (800) 864-1155
Fax: (214) 238-1132

Computer Direct
P.O. Box 55886
Birmingham, AL 35255
Phone: (205) 988-9708
Toll free: (800) 366-0676
Fax: (205) 987-3237

Computer Shopper
One Park Avenue
New York, NY 10016
Phone: (212) 503-3900
Toll free: (800) 274-6384
Fax: (212) 503-3995

Nuts & Volts Magazine
430 Princeland Court
Corona, CA 91719
Phone: (909) 371-8497
Toll free: (800) 783-4624
Fax: (909) 371-3052
http://www.nutsvolts.com

PC Novice Magazine
P.O. Box 85380
Lincoln, NE 68501
Toll Free (800) 472-3500

Processor
P.O. Box 85518
Lincoln, NE 68501
Phone: (402) 479-2141
Toll Free (800) 334-7443
Fax: (402) 477-9252

Software Tools &Diagnostics

BCM Advanced Research

BCM Advanced Research
1 Hughes
Irvine, CA 92716
Phone: (714) 470-1888
Fax: (714) 470-0883
http://www.bcmcom.com

First Aid 95 Deluxe

Software that detects and fixes hundreds of Windows 95 problems.

CyberMedia Inc.
3000 Ocean Park Blvd   Suite 2001
Santa Monica, CA 90405
Phone: (310) 581-4700
Fax: (310) 581-4720
http://www.cybermedia.com

Micro-Scope 6.1

Software that helps you diagnose problems with a PC. This software is works regardless of the operating system which may be installed and checks CPU, memory, IRQs, DMAs, BIOS, hard drives, floppy drives, video cards, more.

Micro 2000
1100 E Broadway   Suite 301
Glendale, CA 91205
Toll-free (800) 864-8008
Phone: (818) 547-0125
Fax: (818) 547-0397
http://www.micro2000.com

PC Snoop

A hard disk and floppy disk diagnostic and repair utility

Computer Intelligence Corp
42015 Ford Rd   Suite 262
Canton, MI 48187-3529
Phone: (313) 981-9630
Fax: (313) 981-9634
http://www.adcomm.com/pcsnoop/

Post-Probe

A plug-in card that helps to troubleshoot problems in "dead" PCs. The LEDs on the card identify problem areas.

Micro 2000
1100 E Broadway   Suite 301
Glendale, CA 91205
Phone: (800) 864-8008
Fax: (818) 547-0397
http://www.micro2000.com

Rescue 95

Windows 95 diagnostic utility package.

Super Win
811 W. 17th. St
Hutchinson, KS 67501
E-mail address: superwin@aol.com
http://members.aol.com/evanetten/
    index.htm

Symantec's

A hard disk and floppy disk diagnostic and repair utility

Symantec
42015 Ford Rd   Suite 262
Canton, MI 48187-3529
Phone: (313) 981-9630
Fax: (313) 981-9634
http://www.adcomm.com/pcsnoop/

Manufacturers & Suppliers

Where can I buy components?

There are loads of places which sell computer components.

Computer Stores

Most local computer stores build custom computers to order. These local computer stores also sell components. Many times these components are of the *OEM* variety, that is they are not packaged in fancy boxes, but are bulk packed to reduce costs. The quality of these components is usually as high as the equivalent retail packaged components.

Computer Superstores

Computer "superstores" such as Best Buy, Circuit City, CompUSA, ElekTek, Frys, Micro Center and others also sell components. These stores usually sell retail packaged components and are noted for competitive prices and quality products and have standard return policies for defective merchandise.

Computer Shows

Another attractive place to buy components is at one of the many computer shows. These are sometimes called expos, fairs, flea markets or swap meets and are held in many cities nationwide, usually on weekends. At these shows, dozens of small hardware and software vendors sell everything from ink refill kits and paper for your printer, to motherboards, memory, add-on cards and complete computer systems, often at deeply discounted prices.

Since most of these vendors participate in the shows regularly and welcome repeat business, they stand behind the quality and performance of the components which they sell. As is the case with all purchases, don't buy a component based solely on its price. Rather, buy a component because it meets your exact requirements and because you feel that a given vendor can meet those needs satisfactorily.

Check your local newspapers and computer bulletin boards for the location of these shows.

Mail Order / Phone Order

You can also buy components from mail order firms. An especially large source of mail order companies is "rags" such as *Computer Shopper* and *Nuts & Volts*. Other monthly magazines have extensive ads from components suppliers. Check these publications to find a list of mail order (and toll free 800 number) hardware component dealers. You can usually buy those "hard to find" components from many of the mail order electronic parts suppliers.

On the next pages is a list of manufacturers and suppliers of components and accessories which you may contact to find out more about their products.

Abrams Computer Industries
444 Lake Cook Road
Suite 1
Deerfield, IL 60015
Phone: (847) 267-0644
Fax: (847) 940-7715
Supplier of motherboards, CPUs (including Cyrix 6x86), memory

Acer Labs

4701 Patrick Henry Drive

Santa Clara, Ca 95054

Phone: (408) 764-0644

Fax: (408) 496-6142

http://www.acer.com

Motherboards and chipsets

Advanced Integration Research

2188 Del Franco Street

San Jose, CA 95131

Phone: (408) 428-0800

Fax: (408) 428-0950

http://www.airwebs.com

Manufacturer of motherboards

Alltech Electronics

2618 Temple Heights

Oceanside, CA 92056

Phone: (619) 724-2404

Fax: (619) 724-8808

http://www.allelec.com

Supplier of electronics components and parts

Alltronics

2300 Zanker Road

San Jose, CA 95131

Phone: (408) 943-9773

Fax: (408) 943-9776

http://www.alltronics.com

Supplier of electronics components and parts

Alternative Computer Solutions

Naperville, IL 60565

Phone: (708) 420-9921

Fax: (708) 420-9312

Supplier of memory

AMD Corporation

One AMD Place

Sunnyvale, CA 94088

Phone: (408) 749-5703

Fax: (408) 774-7024

http://www.amd.com

Manufacturer of CPUs

American Megatrends International

6145-F Northbelt Pkwy

Norcross, GA 30071

Phone: (770) 246-8600

Toll free: 800-U-BUY-AMI

Fax: (770) 246-8790

http://www.megatrends.com

BIOS

Amtech Computers

4005 Carpenter Road

Ypsilanti, MI 48197

Phone: (313) 677-6868

Fax: (313) 677-8778

Supplier of motherboards, CPUs, memory, add-on cards, cases, peripherals

A.R.E. Electronics

15272 State Route 12 East

Findlay, OH 45840

Phone: (419) 422-1588

Fax: (419) 422-4432

Supplier of cables, connectors, tools, switch boxes, hardware.

Astra Computer Corp.

4803 Donald Avenue

Richmond Hts, OH 44143

Phone: (216) 691-9551

Fax: (216) 691-9756

Supplier of motherboards, CPUs, memory, add-on cards, peripherals, cases

ASUS Computers International

721 Charcot Avenue

San Jose, CA 95131

Phone: (408) 474-0567

Fax: (408) 474-0568

http://www.asus.com

Manufacturer of motherboards

Avery Distributors

3685 Stone School Rd

Ann Arbor, MI 48108

Phone: (313) 677-5844

gersha@aol.com

Supplier of memory

Award Software International

777 East Middlefield Rd

Mountain View, CA 94043

Phone: (415) 968-4433

Fax: (415) 968-0774

http://www.award.com

BIOS

Compuparts Laboratory, Inc.

201 E Cripe Street

South Bend, IN 46637

Phone: (219) 243-0421

Fax: (219) 243-0422

Supplier motherboards, CPUs, memory, add-on cards

Cyrix Corporation

P.O. Box 850118

Richardson, TX 75085

Phone: (214) 968-8388

Toll free: (800) 462-9749

Fax: (214) 699-9857

http://www.cyrix.com

Manufacturer of CPUs

Digi-Key Corp.

701 Brocks Ave South

Thief River, MN 56701

Toll-free (800) 334-4530

Fax: (218) 681-3380

Supplier of connectors, cables, tools, electronic components and switches.

Digilink Technology

3050 Lake Lansing Rd
Suite B
East Lansing, MI 48823
Phone: (517) 333-9888
Fax: (517) 333-9988
Supplier of motherboards, memory, add-on cards, peripherals, cases

Discount Computer, Inc.

10021 Telegraph Road
Redford, MI 48239
Phone: (313) 531-3241
Fax: (313) 531-1717
Supplier of motherboards, memory, add-on cards, peripherals, cases

DTK Ltd

1035 Centennial Avenue
Picataway, NJ 08854
Phone: (908) 562-8800
Fax: (908) 562-8400
http://www.dtk.com
Manufacturer of BIOs and motherboards

D.W. Technologies

P.O. Box 4061
Dearborn, MI 48126
Phone: (313) 361-6939
Fax: (313) 361-6939
Supplier of motherboards, CPUs, memory, add-on cards, peripherals.

Expert Computer

14510 11 Mile Road
Warren, MI 48089
Phone: (810) 445-6133
Fax: (810) 455-6132
Supplier of motherboards, CPUs, memory, add-on cards, peripherals, cases

GPC Computers

2240 28th Street SE
Grand Rapids, MI 49508
Phone: (616) 452-8948
Fax: (616) 452-8819
Supplier of motherboards, CPUs, memory, add-on cards, peripherals, cases

Halted Electronics Supply

3500 Ryder Street
Santa Clara, CA 95051
Phone: (408) 732-1573
Toll free: (800) 442-3833
Fax: (408) 732-6428
http://www.halted.com
Supplier of electronics components and parts

Hi-Tech Business Machines

5324 West 79th Street
Indianapolis, IN 46268
Phone: (317) 872-6658
Toll free: (800) 335-8302
http://www.hi-tech.net
Memory, add-on cards, peripherals, cases.

Intel Corporation
2200 Mission College Blvd
Santa Clara, CA 95052
Phone: (408) 528-4725
Fax: (408) 765-9904
Manufacturer of CPUs and chipsets

IQ's Technology
15417 West Warren
Dearborn, MI 48126
Phone: (313) 581-0506
Fax: (313) 581-8841
Supplier of motherboards, memory, add-on cards, peripherals, cases.

JDR Microdevices
1850 South 10th Street
San Jose, CA 95112-4108
Phone: (408) 494-1400
Toll free: (800) 538-5000
Fax: (408) 494-1420
Supplier of hardware, cases, power supplies, keyboards, cables, tools, networking

JK Lee Corporation
1198 E. Dundee Road
Palatine, IL 60067
Phone: (847) 358-7115
Fax: (847) 358-7115
Supplier of memory and CPUs

M Technologies Inc
1931 Hartog Drive
San Jose, CA 95131
Phone: (408) 441-8818
http://www.mtiusa.com
Manufacturer of motherboards

MCM Electronics
650 Congress Park Dr
Centerville, OH 45459-4072
Phone: (513) 434-0031
Toll free: (800) 543-4330
Fax: (513) 434-6959
Supplier of hardware, cases, power supplies, keyboards, cables, tools, networking, electronics parts

Marvic International Inc.
768 East 93rd Street
Brooklyn, NY 11236
Phone: (718) 346-7822
Toll Free: (800) 678-8128
Fax: (718) 346-0438
Supplier of hardware, cases, power supplies, keyboards, cables, tools, networking

Microid Research
2336-D Walsh Ave
Santa Clara, CA 95051
http://www.mrbios.com
Manufacturers of BIOS

Microland Computers
9509 N. Milwaukee Ave
Niles, IL 60714
Phone: (847) 966-2300
Fax: (847) 966-2368
Supplier of motherboards, CPUs, add-on cards

Norton Computer Sytems, Inc.

4129 W Saginaw

Lansing, MI 48917

Phone: (517) 323-3170

Fax: (517) 323-2495

Supplier of cables, connectors, tools, switch boxes, hardware.

Opti, Inc.

2525 Walsh Avenue

Santa Clara, Ca 95051

Phone: (408) 980-8174

Fax: (408) 980-8860

http://www.opti.com

Chipsets

Phoenix Technologies Ltd

2770 De La Cruz

Santa Clara, CA 95050

Phone: (408) 654-9000

Fax: (408) 452-1985

http://www.ptldt.com

BIOS

Prime Electronic Components

150 West Industry Court

Deer Park, NY 11729

Phone: (516) 254-0101

Fax: (516) 242-8995

http://www.imsworld.com/prime/

Supplier of electronics components and parts

RA Enterprises

2260 De La Cruz Blvd

Santa Clara, CA 95050

Phone: (408) 986-8286

Toll free: (800) 801-0230

Fax: (408) 986-1009

Supplier of electronics components and parts

Sam's Computers

5218 Wilson Mills Road

Cleveland, OH 44143

Phone: (216) 449-1107

Fax: (216) 449-3795

Supplier of motherboards, CPUs, memory, add-on cards

Silicon Integrated Systems (SIS)

204 North Wolfe Road

Sunnyvale, CA 94086

Phone: (408) 730-5600

Fax: (408) 730-5639

Manufacturer of chipsets

Skyline Computerware

3749 Grand Blvd

Brookfield, IL 60513

Phone: (708) 387-1064

Fax: (708) 387-1063

Supplier of standoffs and other small hardware, cooling fans, cables, add-on cards

Sky-Tech Computers

28480 Southfield Road

Lathrup Village, MI 48076

Phone: (810) 559-6932

Fax: (810) 559-0827

Supplier of motherboards, CPUs, memory, add-on cards, peripherals, cases

Stone Computer, Inc.

3301 W. Central Avenue

Suite 1-C

Toledo, OH 43606

Phone: (419) 536-5299

Fax: (419) 536-5406

Supplier of motherboards, CPUs, memory, add-on cards, peripherals, cases

Super Micro

2178 Paragon Drive

San Jose, Ca 95131

Phone: (408) 451-1118

Fax: (408) 451-1110

http://www.supermicro.com

Manufacturer of motherboards

The Computer Connection

401 N. Main Street

Polk, OH 44866

Phone: (419) 945-2877

Fax: (419) 945-1342

Supplier of motherboards, CPUs, memory, add-on cards, peripherals, cases

Tynan Computers

1753 S. Main Street

San Jose, CA 95035

Phone: (408) 956-8000

Fax: (408) 956-8044

http://www.tynan.com

Manufacturer of motherboards

Wintergreen Systems, Inc.

3315 W. 96th Street

Indianapolis, IN 46268

Phone: (317) 872-1974

Fax: (317) 872-4686

http://www.in.net/wsi

Supplier of motherboards, CPUs, memory, add-on cards

7

Shopping Check List

7 Shopping Check List

So, you think you're ready to go shopping?

On the next pages, we've made a shopping list. This list will help you organize the features that you want for each of the major components in your system.

You may want to make multiple copies of this list.

CPU (circle desired processor)	Vendor A	Vendor B	Vendor C
Pentium processors P266 P300			
Cyrix 6x86 processors P200 P233 P266	$_____	$_____	$_____

Motherboard select features	Motherboard A		Motherboard B		Motherboard C	
CPU speed to 600 MHz?	❏ Yes	❏ No	❏ Yes	❏ No	❏ Yes	❏ No
Maximum RAM to 128MB?	❏ Yes	❏ No	❏ Yes	❏ No	❏ Yes	❏ No
Handles EDO memory?	❏ Yes	❏ No	❏ Yes	❏ No	❏ Yes	❏ No
Bus type (PCI is recommended)	❏ PCI	❏ VLB	❏ PCI	❏ VLB	❏ PCI	❏ VLB
# of PClor AGP slots						
# of ISA slots						
Cache memory capacity (min. 256K)	❏ Onboard	❏ Separate	❏ Onboard	❏ Separate	❏ Onboard	❏ Separate
I/O on MB or separate I/O card	❏ Onboard	❏ Separate	❏ Onboard	❏ Separate	❏ Onboard	❏ Separate
EIDE for 4 fixed drives	❏ Yes	❏ No	❏ Yes	❏ No	❏ Yes	❏ No
2 floppy drives	❏ Yes	❏ No	❏ Yes	❏ No	❏ Yes	❏ No
2 serial ports (16551 comp.)	❏ Yes	❏ No	❏ Yes	❏ No	❏ Yes	❏ No
I game port	❏ Yes	❏ No	❏ Yes	❏ No	❏ Yes	❏ No
I PS/2 mouse port	❏ Yes	❏ No	❏ Yes	❏ No	❏ Yes	❏ No
BIOS						
Plug 'n Play?	❏ Yes	❏ No	❏ Yes	❏ No	❏ Yes	❏ No
Flash?	❏ Yes	❏ No	❏ Yes	❏ No	❏ Yes	❏ No
Model						
Price	$_____		$_____		$_____	

Main memory RAM	Vendor A			Vendor B			Vendor C		
Type: SIMM DIMM	❏ SIMM	❏ DIMM		❏ SIMM	❏ DIMM		❏ SIMM	❏ DIMM	
Parity?	❏ Yes	❏ No		❏ Yes	❏ No		❏ Yes	❏ No	
Amount 16MB 32MB 128MB	❏ 32 MB	❏ 64 MB	❏ 128 MB	❏ 32 MB	❏ 64 MB	❏ 128 MB	❏ 32 MB	❏ 64 MB	❏ 128 MB
Price	$_____			$_____			$_____		

CPU cooling fan	CPU Fan A	CPU Fan B	CPU Fan C
Model			
Price	$_____	$_____	$_____

Case	Case A		Case B		Case C	
Desktop or Tower	❏ Desktop	❏ Tower	❏ Desktop	❏ Tower	❏ Desktop	❏ Tower
Power supply (230 watt minimum)						
Price	$_____		$_____		$_____	

Keyboard	Keyboard A	Keyboard B	Keyboard C
Style			
Model			
Price	$_____	$_____	$_____

Mouse	Mouse A	Mouse B	Mouse C
Style			
Model			
Price	$_____	$_____	$_____

Video display card	Video card A		Video card B		Video card C	
PCI or AGP	❏ PCI	❏ AGP	❏ PCI	❏ AGP	❏ PC	❏ AGP
DRAM or VRAM	❏ DRAM	❏ VRAM	❏ DRAM	❏ VRAM	❏ DRAM	❏ VRAM
Amount of video memory						
Model						
Price	$_____		$_____		$_____	

Monitor	Monitor A		Monitor B		Monitor C	
Screen size viewing area						
Dot pitch (.28 minimum)						
Refresh rate (70MHz minimum)						
Interlace or non-interlace	❏ Interlace	❏ NI	❏ Interlace	❏ NI	❏ Interlace	❏ NI
Maximum resolution (800 x 600 minimum)						
Energy saving features	❏ Yes	❏ No	❏ Yes	❏ No	❏ Yes	❏ No
Model						
Price	$_____		$_____		$_____	

Sound card	Sound card A		Sound card B		Sound card C	
Plug 'n' Play	❏ Yes	❏ No	❏ Yes	❏ No	❏ Yes	❏ No
Model						
Price	$_____		$_____		$_____	

Modem	Modem A		Modem B		Modem C	
56K Baudrate	❏ Yes	❏ No	❏ Yes	❏ No	❏ Yes	❏ No
Model						
Price	$_____		$_____		$_____	

Floppy drive	Floppy drive A		Floppy drive B		Floppy drive C	
3.5" drive	❏ Yes	❏ No	❏ Yes	❏ No	❏ Yes	❏ No
5.25" drive	❏ Yes	❏ No	❏ Yes	❏ No	❏ Yes	❏ No
Model						
Price	$_____		$_____		$_____	

IDE hard drive	IDE hard drive A	IDE hard drive B	IDE hard drive C
Capacity (5.2GB or higher)			
Access speed (12 ms or less)			
Model			
Price	$_____	$_____	$_____

IDE CD-ROM drive	IDE CD-ROM A	IDE CD-ROM B	IDE CD-ROM C
Access speed (10x speed or higher)			
Model			
Price	$_____	$_____	$_____

Software	Vendor A	Vendor B	Vendor C
MS-DOS 5 or 6.22 on diskette	$_____	$_____	$_____
Windows 95 on CD-ROM	$_____	$_____	$_____